Faith

BROUGHT ME THROUGH—

Fortitude

TAUGHT ME

LaShawn J. Tracy

ISBN 978-1-0980-7176-9 (paperback)
ISBN 978-1-0980-7177-6 (digital)

Christian Faith Publishing, Inc.
832 Park Avenue
Meadville, PA 16335
www.christianfaithpublishing.com

Printed in the United States of America

Faith Brought Me Through

Fear, Fight, Family, Freedom, Forthcomings

To my family and friends.

CONTENTS

ACKNOWLEDGMENTS

A special thank you to my parents, Edwin and Joan Tracy; sisters, Sharon and Marcia Pratt; and niece, Shayna Sanders, for always being there. My children, Kayla and Layden Thompson, and stepchildren, Bryan and Bria Thompson, for giving me a reason to fight. A gratifying thanks to Roxanna Thompson Reid for taking me to the hospital. An appreciative thank you to my brothers, sisters, brothers-in-law and sisters-in-law, nephews, godchildren, and adopted sister, Marilyn and Calvin Givens (sister and brother-in-law), Joan and Vernon Bastian Jr. (sister and brother-in-law), Duane Sr. and Roxanne Pratt (brother and sister-in-law), Evan and Regena Pratt (brother and sister-in-law), Vernice Pratt (brother, deceased), Vincent Pratt, Sr. (brother), Eugene Pratt Sr. (brother, deceased), A. Michael Pratt (brother), Kent Pratt (nephew/godson), Patrick Pratt (nephew), Kevin Pratt (nephew), Tara Givens (niece/goddaughter), and Dena (French) Wesley for coming whenever you see I need you. A heartfelt thank you to the bone marrow transplant nursing staff, cancer doctors at the University of Maryland Medical Center in Baltimore, Maryland, infusion nurses and nurse practitioners in the Greenebaum Cancer Center, Dr. Maria Baer, and NP Mike Tidwell (deceased). Lastly, to my extended family, Beulah Baptist Church Family, Smithfield, Pennsylvania, Kamila Johnson, Marian "Ms. Cookie" Mann, Michael Jones Jr., Kirsten Clark, LaRone Clark, Eddie Pace, Frances J. Rollins, Deborah Hall, Pastor Damian Briggs (Eastern Community Church), Kelvin Thompson, Dorothy (Barksdale) Council, Deacon William Bryant (past president, Pennsylvania Baptist Convention), Roy and Talitha Cowan, mentors Pastor Darin Freeman Sr., Carol Powers (deceased), Linda Keys, and all who have helped me over the years become the individual I am. To all those who prayed for my deliverance and kept me lifted up in the name of Jesus Christ, who is my holding and sounding grace through a card, gifts, telephone call, or visit, I want to acknowledge you and say with all my heart, "Thank you!"

TRIBUTE SONG

Chorus: If it wasn't for faith, I don't know what I'd do;
Because faith brought me through some of the tough
times, I thought I knew
If it wasn't for faith, I don't know what I'd do;
All the pain I endured only my faith kept me secure
If it wasn't for faith, I don't know what I'd do;
When at times I never knew what was happening
could have been so true
If it wasn't for faith, I don't know what I'd do.

Verses:

1. Faith is not new. When I fall faith is the only thing that
can catch me and bring me back to what I knew. Faith
was there when it was impossible to believe the situation I seemed to perceive. Once I grabbed a hold of
my faith, I knew I could conquer everything I needed
to reach that ultimate goal. (survival)

Chorus

2. Through it all I never forgot who was in charge of my
life and could do it all in one strife. Faith is priceless;
that only my provider can dismiss my lost direction
and bring me back to my conception. Faith is with me
always because I believe that no matter what may be
thrown my way my faith is here to stay.

Chorus

3. Faith is only a five-letter word that has traveled
miles away to bring fierce aspiration to inspire
one's triumph to heal. So through all my obstacles and strengths that are left at a place. I can
only imagine what more of this road I must take
to make people know that my faith will make no
mistake.

Chorus

LaShawn J. Tracy

INTRODUCTION

I am writing this book as a testimony to what I have been through and to where I am going. I pray it will touch at least one person's heart who may be going or who has already gone through some of my story. I believe stories are just that—a story; but a life story is more like a legend that only the person who goes through it can tell.

Do you find yourself thinking that you don't have a life story because you have not been through a horrific storm? Your story does not always have to be something bad but a testimony for others to hear or read because they may be in a similar predicament. That's the meaning of this book! I want you to relate however you see fit.

You will find out how my unique story can relate to your situation in one way or another. It's not just for you but for those individuals you may come across with testimonies of their own and need gratification that they are doing the right thing. Everything you do in life has a purpose, and that will be addressed in my story. There's not always a reason you can see, but it will be revealed somehow.

I pray that through my story about who I am, my family dynamics, motherhood, the obstacles I've been through, and where I'm about to go will help you understand why it was so important for me to tell my story. No, it's not for everyone! However, for those of you who take the time to read it, I believe it will give you a better understanding of how my faith is the most essential part of who I am, and how I can share it with others through my actions, not just words. I look for the words in this book to be a resource that you can read over and over again when you see you need it the most.

Enjoy the reading and try to put yourself in my shoes. Somehow you may be able to relate when you think there is no way out. Please go and spread some love, respect, and devotion to others as someone may have done for you!

FOCUS OF FAITH

*Stand in faith even when you're having
the hardest time of your life.*

—Unknown

ASSURANCE

When you look at life through my mind, body, and soul, you will find that there is no greater love of mine than having faithfulness. The word *faith* has many meanings or feelings in light of its perception. In the dictionary http://www.merriam-webster.com/info/copyright.htm (2015), *faith* is defined as: "strong belief or trust in someone or something; belief in the existence of God; strong religious feelings or beliefs; and a system of religious beliefs." The origin of *faith* is from Middle English *feith,* from Anglo-French *feid, fei,* from Latin *fides*—akin to Latin *fidere* to trust. Its first known use was in the thirteenth century.

In my experience, faith is love, respect, a comforter, justice, hope, dreams, acknowledgments, accepting failure, dedication, a mysterious indulgence in something you can't touch, see, hear, feel, or smell. This faith gives me a gift that could only come from something imaginary. It is something that you perceive to be true. It is real!

Faith allows me to envision how individuals perceive me or characterize me. It is a tool that helps guide my actions and direction. It grants me with talents and favors that are unique just for me. Faith brings good things when I have patience and perseverance. It sees my strengths and weaknesses I must uphold. It allows me to trust and believe in things I can't see. Faith is not superficial or materialistic. It is a sacrifice we all are born into, but strong beliefs are what enhances it.

It is not something to be played with or defined indirectly. When I have firsthand knowledge of a situation, it opens doors that I probably wouldn't have noticed. For example, it could be when my eyes see darkness, and with my heart, I can see the light. It is just that simple! It is a great insight to how, what, when, where, and why. If I had to live without faith, I don't think I would have made it thus far. It gives me the strength of ten men, kindheartedness, liberation, and to be avid about the road he has made me travel in such a short time in my life.

Faith, to me, isn't something recognizable at first glance. It can make you have blinders on that only you can see through. If you are not careful, it can make you accept the things you would not usually accept. Faith is tricky and only those who believe can associate themselves with the goodness that it brings. So faith can either make you or break you depending on your how, what, when, where, and why it is happening. My faith gives me assurance! It keeps my head out of the clouds and looking toward the light. Faith is my gift to believe there is something greater out there for me. Without my faith, who would I be!

Actually at the age of thirteen, I accepted Jesus Christ as my Lord and Savior and had been baptized to join the choir at Beulah. However, when I put my foot in that water, it felt like my soul was taken out. I was so nervous! Now what did I get myself into? Then I realized it was the Holy Spirit taking over my soul and cleansing me of any impurities. I thought to myself, *Do I really have that many impurities at thirteen years old?* It was a life-changing experience for me that I really adhere too! I did not play with faith, and I do not play with faith. I always kept the faith that God would do many things with me, even if I did not know what to do with them. I had big dreams!

All the things I have experienced in my life, I can't complain or explain. There's always those people, places, or things that help having faith in a higher power more promising, testimony more understandable, accounts more recognizable. For me, it's having the belief that my flesh has done all it can do, but when my faith in the Holy Spirit steps in, I have the supremacy and strength to do all things through Christ.

Stuart Scott, ESPN anchor (2014) gave a great quote to live by, "When you die, it does not mean that you lose to cancer. You beat cancer by how you live, why you live, and in the manner in which you live." This was nothing but faith that kept him comfortable with having cancer and going through the storm. In my opinion, these words were his testimony of how his faith kept him. For everyone fighting a fight, no matter if it's a terminal illness, a mental illness, a community illness, a societal illness, or an undetermined illness, believing in something greater than man will always keep you strong.

So as I journey through this life, I know that my flesh may not be able to endure all the obstacles that are in store, but my faith will overpower anything my flesh may not have an answer for. As I say, the people you think have your best interest at heart may just be sucking all the energy out of your soul. But faith will give you the recharge that you need to be restored. Fortunately since I have the Holy Spirit in me, nothing is going to keep me down. I sometimes wonder what the future has in store for me, but if I keep my eyes on God, everything is under control.

Faith is my testimony that there is a better place for me. That what I imagine can come true. That no matter how I characterize myself, I will always be me. That when this life here on earth is over, I am a person who lived life through faith. That is why I am still breathing so that I can change at least one person's perception of faith. That where I stand, faith will stand also. Faith is such a miraculous belief and perception. Just try it, and you will see!

No, I would never declare myself a pastor, priest, bishop (as they are fondly being called today), minister, deacon, deaconess, evangelist, or any high authority in the house of the Lord. I am just a messenger to make sure that His message touches the right eyes, ears, hands, and mouth. I am just a vessel!

See, I do not feel that today's churches are properly displaying what the Lord has entrusted in us to deliver. As a black woman, church has always been where we were to take all our burdens and leave them there (as the saying goes). Not in today's black churches or churches, period!

They make you question if faith is something to believe in or justify as a belief. Our ancestors used faith as their guide to survive in this cruel world, and that is being mocked today, in my opinion. We have many people playing church and not being about the Word. Yes, the Bible was written by man, but in the church, it is a guide/recipe for us to use in our steps toward deliverance.

Funny though, when faith does come in to show up and show out, let's see how many of these good "cherch" folks are really going to be left standing. No, I would never judge a person because my belief tells me there is only *one* who can be the judge. I just speculate (thinking)!

As you can tell, I am one who carries faith with me every minute, hour, second of the day. I have no fear because faith is with me always. This is what I have used to make it.

While going through what I would say was my most trivial experience I have faced thus far, I kept good spirits the entire time. In my marriage, in the hospital, through cancer treatment, in my divorce, and as a single mother, I had the faith to smile!

It always makes me smile because while I was in the hospital at UMMC, the nurses would come to my room so that I could brighten up their days because I was always smiling no matter what obstacle I had to overcome. They would tell me they wished all the patients were like me. I would say, "There's only one of me!" (still smiling). I was determined to make the best of my situation, no matter what the consequences. My faith in God was going to bring me through, and I never second-guessed (giving praise).

It's kind of interesting, if I must say so myself (smiling), because I walk with the faith of God in my heart and with my guardian angels on both sides through it all. What some may see as obstacles, I see another opportunity to make things better! I believe that the Holy Spirit has given me the confidence I need to keep being assertive to try to be better tomorrow than I was today. It's not an easy road or walk or run (whichever you prefer), but it is what I use to keep me lifted up.

Some may agree to disagree, but one thing is for sure—He is waking me up every morning so that I can go out and make one more effort to do what it is He has for me to do. I just give all praise and thanks in believing that faith is omnipotent. One thing for sure and two things are for certain, if you carry the faith, you will have church anytime and anywhere! Just try it (maturity)!

WHO AM I?

I'd rather be hated for who I am,
than loved for who I am not.

—Jory Hancock

I was born on Saturday, October 19, 1974, to Edwin and Joan. I have four (three deceased) brothers and four sisters. It was eleven children to my mom's previous marriage and then came me to the current reunion. My father only has me (smile). There are five years between me and Vernice; ten years between me and Joan; Marcia is twenty-two years my senior; Eugene Sr. (deceased) was twenty-one years my elder; all the other fall in between. I was born into a large loving family. Therefore, family makes me happy! Not a lot of people can say this, but I can, and you will see why.

So why not start by learning about who I am through my name—LaShawn—and why it fits me so well! As I researched it, I found out many things about why my name makes me so special and things I did not necessarily know about myself (intriguing.) First, I am a very outgoing, friendly (family may disagree), and a charming person who loves to perform and see the reaction of the crowd by making them laugh; and most importantly, I inspire them. Although performing is a hard thing to do, and I do it so naturally, it's hard not to be impressed (talent I just recognized.) By growing up with low self-esteem, it causes you to oversee some of your talents as I did. I am a very inspiring person and should be proud of myself!

Second, I am a left-brained person which means I am a smart scientist. My left side is dominant which makes me a logical, analytical, and objective person. I love to live in a well-organized world and base my assumptions on logic and critical thinking. My strengths are working with numbers, mathematical reasoning, and a well-developed language. I have very strong arguments when it comes to debating a problem or picking sides and can usually convince others to take my point. My intelligence and work ethic can change the world through some scientific breakthroughs (which I'm working on!).

Third, when you think about me, the first thing that comes to mind is my sweet caring nature and loyalty. Everyone knows when I say something, I really mean it and am always the first person that friends turn to whenever they need a little advice or a shoulder to cry on. Although it might take a little while for me to get to know you, once I do, I am a fiercely loyal friend for life.

Next, my past lives have been full of love, lust, romance, and passion. I am irresistible (ego)! I have a zest for life that few can match. I live every moment to its fullest, and I am a sucker for all things sensual. I racked up the love points and never second-guess myself (mostly) and always pursue the romance of my wildest dreams! I am here to love and be loved! Then again, the word that best describes me is *tenacious*. I am strong, resilient, persistent, and unbendable. I have been through plenty of struggles in my life, but I have never let anyone keep me down. I firmly believe you make your own destiny, and I've worked hard to pave my own path.

So you can guess that the mystery behind my name is that I am a bit of a wild child, always trying something new and doing things I'm scared of. I may make risky decisions at times, but one thing is for sure—my life could never be called boring! I believe that life is too short to stay in my comfort zone all the time, and true growth comes from challenging my perceived limits.

My superhero and supernatural powers are healing. I am a hero that recovers quickly from combat injuries and have the ability to heal any wound others might have. I am a counselor and friend that always helps others, and in a fantasy world, I would be immortal with some effort that could bring others back to life.

I am extremely original and one of the most original individuals out there. If there was an international sign for originality, it would have my face on it (cheese). I am different from the average person, not only by looks and behavior but by thought. I love to face new challenges and think outside the box when it comes to solving problems! Sometimes it's hard for others to understand the way I think, and this may cause conflicts; but in the end, I am the one that has the power to change the world! For this reason, my nickname should be Punkin because I am sweet, and when people see me, they just want to pinch my adorable cheeks (don't do it) and give me huge hugs because I spread love.

Therefore, the scripture that best describes me is Psalm 91 because I am a protective-warrior type who is not afraid to stand up to the darkness of this world. It is known as the Soldier's Prayer. I am a soldier in the fight for what's right and making sure the right way wins. My inspirational quote is to put your heart, mind, and soul into even your smallest acts. "This is the secret of success" (Swami Sivananda 2015).

If I had wings, they would be a griffin (a mythical creature with the head and wings of an eagle and the body of a lion, typically depicted with pointed ears and with the eagle's legs taking the place of the forelegs) (Wikipedia 2015)! A sense of duality within me, ranging from qualities of kindness and sensitivity to ferociousness and vengeance. One side of these wings depict the noble and more just side of your tendencies; I can be extremely loyal and gentle to those I guard and connect with. However, when someone decides to cross me or harm another I care deeply about, I become a force no one wants to reckon with (true talk). I remain protective either way and primarily symbolize strength and trust above all else. I expect others to live up to these standards and not just myself.

Since I have several ways to show myself, it would be permissive to say the natural disaster I would be is an earthquake because I don't yell a lot (my children think different, smile). I keep my anger inside, and only those who really know me can tell when the crack starts to show. When I am angry, it's usually in a subtle way because I hate confrontation, and it takes a lot to crack my cool.

I am leader material! I think of things I can implement each day in my work to raise my confidence, increase my courage, enhance my communication, and strengthen my character. I talk to the people around me that are strong role models for character-based leadership traits. I look for ways to emulate what I see in these leaders and follow in their footsteps, one step at a time (not literally).

I am a woman who guys look at and automatically have some sort of attraction to (ego). I am slightly girly, fun, and always polite. A lot of the time, I play hard to get but secretly may have a crush on the guy too. I am a strong believer in Jesus Christ and am not afraid to let others know. I take pride in my religion and grow as God wants me to.

What makes me happy is family. My parents, siblings, aunt, uncles, and grandparents have all played a part in making me who I am, and nothing makes me happier than some family time. I am very close to my family. I love getting together for holidays and calling them throughout the week. I believe strongly that nothing is as important as family.

FANTASY WORLD

I would be a titan! I am a god much larger than life, ruler of the sky and the earth. In a fantasy realm, I have the final say of all those who worship me, although I never take advantage of their kind. I have incredible strength and come from a legend of divinity, often influencing the mortals beneath me with my guidance and leadership. There are those who challenge my authority and want to overthrow me, but I never back down from a fight; it's just not my style.

So now that you know me a little better, let's talk about my family dynamics and the impact it had on my life as a youngster. Family is a major part of my early existence. You will be amazed with what you will find out. Let's go!

THE DYNAMICS OF FAMILY

*In each family a story is playing itself out, and
each family's story embodies its hope and despair.*

—Auguste Napier

My family dynamics is a little captivating to say the least. They all play a role in how our family functions as a whole and how their characters, trials, and characteristics have had an impact on the lives of so many who follow. We have secrets, just like the next family, but we learn from them and not allow them to interfere with the dynamics of our family.

Let me start with my parents since they are part of the reason we exist. Then I am going to address my siblings in order and explain how I view each of them. Now all of us are very unique. A few of them stand out in my life more than others, but they all have played a role in my upbringing and life in general. I would be premised to say that they haven't been the reason I value family. I will also touch a little on the twelve nieces and nephews who grew up with me.

My parents, Edwin and Joan, are special within their own rights. They have raised beautiful children who all contribute a little something to society. Although my dad did not raise many of my siblings, he is the only father figure that they have had in their lives consistently for over forty years. See, my mom was married, when she was sixteen years old, to a man who was physically and mentally abusive to her, and unfortunately, some of that trickled down to her children. However, when my dad came along, he promised her that he would protect her and her children and not to worry (he does not believe in putting your hands on women or vice versa). With that said, let's start by talking about my dad first since the man is the head of the family.

My dad is a quiet, stubborn, devoted, introvert, athletic, and charismatic man. He loves the outdoors and can sit in any temperature for long periods of time (now that he is getting older with arthritis, he can't as much, but he still does.) My dad was a very good football player and could have gone to the pros; but during that period, blacks had many struggles with racial bias, and my dad did not think he was the right man for that job. He is very strong and sometimes does not know his own strength (laughing). He would break almost everything he tried to fix. My dad played golf, softball with the church, bowling, went fishing and hunting as I was growing up. He worked in the coal mines most of my younger years. In my eyes, he is a very special man to have taken the responsibility of marrying a woman who had already been married with eleven children, and he had none. Edwin treats us basically all the same, except he wants the men to be men and not boys (something they really haven't been taught). My dad is very verbal when he has been sipping on that "apple juice." I would say he has an addiction, but he would totally disagree. He is a man of little words, but if my dad likes you, he likes you; and if he does not, he does not, no filter at all. I think he is a little misunderstood because he carries many weights that he will not reveal. If anything, I would say my dad is a great man who loves his family.

Now Joan, on the other hand, has become a "pistol". She doesn't take mess from no one anymore. When she left her first marriage, she promised to never put herself or her children in that situation again. My mom had some rough times in her marriage after her father passed because her husband was ten years her elder and thought he had the power to control her. But my mom always had a mind that could outsmart you even when you thought you had her trapped (a very smart lady). My mom used to say that since she did not graduate from high school, she didn't think she was smart, but raising children without having a mother of her own, she did a very good job. One unique characteristic about my mom is that she is not a quitter! My mom is a very loving, outspoken, honorable, resilient, stubborn, clever, a little introverted and extroverted at times, God-fearing, and respectful lady. She went from a father who gave her anything she wanted to a husband who was abusive (first marriage) and has developed strength through the Lord Jesus Christ and her children. She always says her children are her best friends. My mom is very prideful, protective of her babies, and she lets everyone know ("These are all my babies!"). She will travel to the ends of the earth for her babies and will dare you to question her actions. I think she treats the boys like babies and the girls are taught to be independent. This will show up when I address my siblings. My mom is the pillar of our family, and she doesn't take no for an answer. I have noticed that with age, her patience level is becoming intolerable with certain people and circumstances. One thing about my mom is that she stresses and worries a lot, and in some cases, she has no control over the situation (Scorpio trait). But anyone who meets her will fall in love with her because of her pleasant spirit. She is a dynamic woman with very domineering ways and has a way with all her children that only her children understand.

So as she would have it, our family dynamics is somewhat domineering with respect to birth order and individuality. All of us have a talent or gift that we have been passing down through generations (some good and some bad)! Some of us display more actions than others, but they are all significant in the way we respect our family. Most of them have a memory that's out of this world. So understanding our birth order, spacing, family size, and gender effect on our personality formation and behavior will give you a more concise picture of our dynamics.

In our large family, we have large gaps between each group of children which affects our birth order. For every three-to-four-year gap, the cycle changes. Then the gap changes if there are five or more years which means that child may be considered the firstborn or only child. Since this gap pertains to me, I would have both. The gender of us also plays a role in behavior and personality. For example, Sharon is the second child in the second cycle, but she acts like the firstborn. You will see what I'm talking about in my descriptions. The most interesting fact about our birth order is that the children begin with a girl and ends with a girl, and the grandchildren begin with a boy and ends with a boy since we are all done having children.

How ironic, huh? Now for the great-grands and great-great-grands, only time will tell because my two children are the youngest, and they are growing up with their second and third cousins. I can say that this lineage will go on and on and on.

Therefore, our large family of twelve children has four gap cycles between the brothers and sisters. The grandchildren are too many to count (giggle.) The first group is the first three children (Marcia, Eugene, and Duane); the second group: Mike, Sharon, Marilyn, Vincent, Scott, Joan; the third group: Evan and Vernice; and the last group is me. Our personalities are very significant in the birth order. The firstborns are responsible, assertive, task-oriented, perfectionistic, and supporters of authority. They have higher academic achievement and poses leadership abilities. The second born, which is a girl, shares the personality of the firstborn. The middle children feel inferior to the older child or forgotten, so they try to rebel or misbehave in order to draw attention to themselves. The last-born child is considered the baby, and our large families, they develop strong social and coping skills. Some may have self-esteem problems if power is taken away but use the powerlessness into a personal asset by becoming the boss of the family, coyly eliciting or openly demanding their own way. The only child grows up relating to adults in the family but have trouble relating to peers. However, this changes as they reach adulthood and get along well with adults. Only children are achievement-oriented and most likely to attain academic success and attend college. They may also be creative. But only children can be pampered and spoiled as last born and can be self-centered. They sometimes please others if it suits them but may also be uncooperative. They can also be overprotected. Some only children become hypercritical, not tolerating mistakes or failure in themselves or others. They can also transform this perfectionist tendency into rescuing behavior, agonizing over the problems of others, and rushing to take over and solve everything without letting others help themselves (www.healthofchildren.com/B/Birth-Order.html 2015). So here we go!

Firstborn (first child) Marcia has three boys: two biological and a nephew of Vernice's she raised. She was married at twenty years old to a man who was physically, mentally, and emotionally abusive. He was an alcoholic who tried to control her. Marcia left her marriage, never to return after ten years. She was a straight-A student but had to work hard for it. Marcia only stands 4'11" but has a heart of a lion. She went to California University of Pennsylvania to receive her bachelor's and master's degree. Her first and only marriage made her resilient, aggressive, strong-minded, and arrogant. She is retired as the associate dean at Seton Hill College in Greensburg, Pennsylvania. She is also a deacon at our home church in Pennsylvania. Marcia loves to watch sports (all sports). She is smart, observant, conservative, and a perfectionist. Some of us refer to her as our mother (smiling) because she is so close in age to our mother and acts like our mother at times. One thing I wish Marcia would have achieved was her doctorate degree because she went through all the coursework but did not want to write the dissertation. She could be Dr. Deacon Marcia who currently resides in Greensburg, Pennsylvania.

Middle child (second child) Eugene "Gene" (deceased) was one year younger than Marcia. He had nine children: two to his first wife; two random; three to another woman; and two stepchildren with his second wife. Gene married his first wife when he was eighteen years old and stayed married to her for twenty-two years. He married his second wife in 1994 and he was still married when he passed away. Gene was a lady's man and wasn't ashamed to say it (obviously.) He lived in Detroit, Michigan, and could dress for success. He was a very hard worker, arriving at work three to four hours before time and never missing work. Gene was not physically abusive, but with all his women on the side and having five children in those affairs, he was emotionally abusive to his first wife and her children. He graduated from high school and obtained a certificate in computer but never specialized in it (a skill that would be very useful today.) He considered himself as a salesman for over twenty years and pursued careers in Kinney's shoes and later as a used car salesman. He had chronic obstructive pulmonary disease (COPD) which is a group of lung diseases that block airflow and make it difficult to breathe (yes, he was a smoker). He always wanted to be recognized as the *big* brother. Gene was also a deacon. He was clever, wise, talkative, charming, arrogant, selfless and self-serving, and demanding. The older he got, the more antisocial he became (a genetic trait, I believe, from his father whom he did not like.) Gene acted more like his father than he wanted to admit, but he was always my big brother who I could talk to about anything, and he would give it to me straight up to the day he passed on July 3, 2016. He died from a complication of a study they were trying for patients with COPD to open up their lungs with splints, but it was unsuccessful for Gene; but I believe he knew that was his last hope to breathe on his own without the oxygen tank. Gene was sixty-three years old. I loved Gene, and I am still trying to cope with his passing.

Last born (third child) Duane is three years younger than Gene. He has seven children: three to his first wife; two random; and two to his current marriage. Duane is one of those people you love to hate, as the saying goes. When he was younger, he was an alcoholic and very abusive physically and mentally to both of his wives and children. He used to force his children to eat large plates of food and discipline them if they didn't (only the first three children). I don't think of him as a lady's man, but I guess in a way, he was. He was very aggressive, mean, clever, and arrogant. He is a veteran of the United States Army and a certified mechanic. Duane resided most of his life in Pittsburg, Pennsylvania, before moving to Ohio for seven years. That's where he turned his life over to Jesus Christ. He returned to Uniontown, Pennsylvania and became a deacon of our home church. He has changed in so many ways, especially with his family. Duane has always been family-oriented. He currently works for Duquesne Light in Pittsburgh, Pennsylvania, owns several rental properties, and an automechanic shop in Uniontown, Pennsylvania. He works hard, very playful, sarcastic, sociable, hell-raiser, assertive, and devoted. Duane admits he has done things in his past he is not proud of but tries every day to be better than the day before. He knows he cannot change the past or erase any harsh feelings, but he is trying to be a better man for his grandchildren. Duane has always been an older brother who demands that his little sister be very independent when it comes to cars and men. If I ever need anything, I can call on Duane, and he will be there in two shakes (literally). Duane resides with his wife in Uniontown, Pennsylvania. He gets his playfulness from his father and just adores his mommy. I think he puts our mom right after God in his eyes—that's how much he loves and adores her.

Firstborn (fourth child) Anthony "Mike" Esq. is four years younger than Duane. He has three children. His first child, he had at fifteen years old, and his other two children are to his ex-wife. Mike is a lady's man as well. He tries not to act like the rest of his family, but he is no different. We are all cut from the same cloth (smile). No, he has never been abusive to any woman in any way, which is a blessing. However, bringing different women around isn't displaying a good role model behavior for his nephews or son. Mike never really had time for family because he always had obligations which prevented him from attending many family functions over the years. He currently is a corporate attorney and shareholder for Greenberg Traurig LLP and former corporate attorney and partner for Pepper Hamilton law firm both located in Philadelphia, Pennsylvania and holds many memberships of many organizations for humanity. Mike is formerly known as the first black Pennsylvania Turnpike commissioner. He was an exceptional athlete and student in high school and college playing basketball and football, winning many trophies and awards. He can sing and is a great public speaker. Mike is charming, intelligent, arrogant, confident, sociable, a braggart, and logical. He has a way with him that others seem to find interesting, especially in politics. To his family, he is just Mike, no big deal at all. Now that he is older, he is becoming more family-oriented. I never had a real close relationship with Mike, even though I think he tried. He was always the sibling I wanted to outdo when I grew up as far as academics. I figured if education got him this far, how far will it get me (thinking)? He was my challenge, but he never knew. Mike currently resides in Philadelphia, Pennsylvania with his new wife, Barbara.

Second born (fifth child) Sharon is eleven months younger than Mike. They are the same age for four days (how about that?). She has three children to her ex-husband and high school boyfriend. Sharon was physically and mentally abused by her ex-husband who had problems with substance abuse, cheating, and alcohol. He was very controlling when it came to Sharon in every aspect. He didn't want her to work so she could have her own money to provide for her children. This made Sharon seem very passive and detached from him. She played more mind games and had mind control like no other and still does. They moved around a lot for his job, so they never really felt like anywhere was home until they moved to Connecticut. He never had a bond with Shayna (their oldest and only daughter) which bothered Sharon, but they were very close. Shayna was very protective of her mother at a young age and still is today.

When he mistreated Shayna by making her walk ten blocks to school and did not give her lunch money, that was the final draw. She left and never looked back. Sharon is the type where she will let you mess with her because she can usually outsmart you, but don't mess with the ones she loves because she turns into a beast. I respect her fully because she had to learn how to do everything because her ex controlled all the finances, but she was no dummy. Sharon became obsessive-compulsive, apathetic, and no-nonsense after her separation and divorce of twenty-six years. She currently holds a BS degree in social work and works as a paraprofessional with special education students for the New Britain public school system, New Britain, Connecticut. She is very family-oriented. She acts like she doesn't love children, but she has a way with children that most can't understand. Sharon is an introvert, confident, arrogant, aggressive, domineering, and fun. She can always find a way to make me smile, no matter how she might feel. She is one of my siblings I shared my upbringing with because she was always there. Sharon resides in New Haven, Connecticut with her daughter.

Middle child (sixth child) Marilyn is one year younger than Sharon. She has two children and a stepson. She is definitely one of a kind. Marilyn is the outgoing radical sister who has tried almost everything. She got pregnant with Patrick at sixteen years old and was not allowed any medication because she wasn't supposed to get pregnant. However, Patrick was raised by his grandparents and aunts. He moved with Marilyn once he got older, but it was short-lived. Marilyn was diagnosed with stage 3 breast cancer at thirty-two years old which she beat and currently has acute lupus which is an everyday struggle. She worked in customer service for Verizon before her illness where she met her husband. Marilyn really acts her place as the middle child of the family—it's all about Marilyn. She is egocentric, stubborn, clever, charming, outgoing, talkative, arrogant, anxious, opinionated, inquisitive, and uneasy. She holds grudges, center of attention, and is self-serving. She is the only sibling who is outgoing and has friends (can't really understand that situation). Our relationship is more one-sided because you have to meet Marilyn where she is to cope. I wouldn't change her for anything. Marilyn resides in Washington, DC, and her ex-husband resides in District Heights, Maryland.

Seventh child, Vincent, is eleven months younger than Marilyn, and they are the same age for ten days. He has seven children: five from his first wife and two random. Vincent was very mean, angry, aggressive, detached, boastful, abusive, alcoholic, and domineering. He was with his first wife for twenty-three years. He had some terrible boys which stemmed from his behaviors and actions. I believe he had his reasons, but they were not the proper way to raise boys back then. Vincent lived in the Cleveland, Ohio, area for over twenty-five years until he became ill and moved to Uniontown, Pennsylvania. He is very nervous, a chain-smoker, observant, and self-serving. Vincent is currently disabled but has a hobby for fixing computers. He changed when my brother Scott died and has never been the same since. Vincent's bond with me is different than my other siblings because we just talk when we need to. It really is an indescribable relationship, but it's all in love. Vincent resides in Uniontown, Pennsylvania.

Eighth child, Scott (deceased), is one year younger than Vincent. They were thick as thieves. Scott had one child. He was very daring, slick, funny, and a con artist. Scott was wise beyond his years, and he knew it. He and Vincent were thick as thieves. They went to the military together but was dishonorably discharged because Scott fell asleep at his post (giggle). So he and Vincent both left (shaking my head). Since I was so little when he passed, all I know is that he was my cool brother with no worries. Scott was very intellectual, clever, playful, confident, and arrogant. He was shot in the back of the head on August 19, 1981, at the age of nineteen, by the next-door neighbor when he lived in Detroit, Michigan. It is still hard for me to talk about Scott till this day!

Last born (ninth child) Joan is one year younger than Scott. She is the only one named after our mom. She has two children and four grandchildren. Joan has been with the same man since she was eighteen years old. They have been abusive to each other for most of that time. Joan was the one who put her husband, Vernon, before her family which she was supposed to, but that's not how our dynamics really work. She never let her children be around the family without her supervision until her daughter turned sixteen years old and out of control. Joan and her husband were very overprotective of their children. Her husband had total control over her emotionally and mentally. She could do nothing without him. It's hasn't been until recently that she has the courage to stand up for herself and not be scared. Joan holds a child development certificate in preschool, ninety hours in childcare, and a director's credential in childcare with the state of Maryland. She has worked in childcare for over twenty years in many areas but, most significantly, as a teacher. Joan is very crafty and can make the most interesting gifts. She has really matured and found her place in life because of her grandchildren. Joan is uneasy, anxious, passive, creative, a comedian, well organized, clever, and free-spirited. She has grown over the years to be confident, talkative, sociable, adventurous, and demanding. As the sister closest to me, our bond is growing. Joan resides in Frederick, Maryland, with her husband and children.

Firstborn (tenth child) Evan is three years younger than Joan. He has six children: two from his first wife, two random, and two stepchildren. He has been married three times and is still currently married to his third wife. Evan was Vernice's big brother and best friend! Evan was not an abusive individual, he always took the high road and ceased conflict before it happened. However, Evan was very quiet and observant which gave off the impression that he was aggressive. He never really got upset unless you messed with his family, but still it was kind of a calming action. He was a great basketball player in high school and some college. Evan is currently one of the directors for the American Red Cross chapter in Philadelphia, Pennsylvania. He has worked many jobs over the years and has been very successful at them. He is family-oriented, very neat, well organized, pays a lot of attention to detail, charming, smart, hardworking, creative, arrogant, and easygoing. Evan has always been the brother you can talk to about anything, and he would tell you just what to do—no questions asked and gets the job done. He is stubborn, jack-of-all-trades, sociable with those he knows, and observant. He protected his little brother, Vernice, at no cost. The older he gets, the more outspoken and demanding he is becoming. Evan resides with his wife in Philadelphia, Pennsylvania.

Last born (eleventh child), Vernice (deceased), is two years younger than Evan. He had seven children which he would comment that they all were not his but that they were blamed on him (laughing). Always wondered about that, huh! Vernice was physically and mentally abusive to his girlfriends in his early years, mainly because they would pick with him, and he had a short fuse when it came to nonsense. He always questioned who his father was, but he acted just like my father in so many ways. Vernice was very unsettled with not believing who his father was, and I believe it caused many of his aggressive actions. He had the same father as the rest of my siblings though. Evan was the only person who could calm Vernice down (smile). He had a lot of aggression, and it was obvious after our brother Scott was killed. He had many girlfriends but never wanted to get married (never asked why). Vernice was a jack-of-all-trades but very good at carpentry, especially laying carpet and floors. He loved his family. He was creative, daring, stubborn, confident, smart, annoyed, and free-spirited. Vernice was an alcoholic but encouraged his nephews not to be like him in that respect. He lived life to its fullest and made sure he took care of his family any way he knew how. Although he was my older brother, I was more like the older sister (smile). Vernice and I were only five years apart, but it seemed like we lived in two different eras. He died on May 19, 2011, from lung cancer at forty-one years old. I loved Vernice and miss him every day!

Firstborn and only child (twelfth child) is me. I am five years younger than Vernice. I am my father's only child. I have two children from my ex-husband. You already read my characteristics. I am the youngest but feel like the oldest at times because I am always called upon, even by my mom (strange, right?). I believe it's because I am more like her when it comes to certain things, and I use logic, not emotion. Well, that's my story, and I am sticking with it (giggling). I may be the next in line (shrugging shoulders), I guess, to be the pillar of the family (which I don't know why because I'm still learning [smile]). I do it all out of love! You will find out more about me throughout my legend.

As for the twelve nieces and nephews that grew up with me, many of their behaviors and actions are learned. I don't believe my brothers were the best role models for this generation, but the sisters picked up where they could. Each one has a trait or characteristic of their grandmother (my mom). Although we were tight as thieves when we were little, we kept each other in check. I was the auntie, and they knew it, but they treated me just like a sister. It was odd at times, but we had fun. They had much respect for me as I did for them! In each of them, I can see humbleness, compassion, devotion, determination, and arrogance which is how I described most of my siblings and mom. One thing is for sure, they may have strayed into their own individual personalities, but life somehow brought some of them back to what they know is right, no matter how long it took. They definitely had a praying grandmother!

So it is perceived that my family plays an important part of my upbringing and eccentric style. Our dynamics are of many colors and shades, just like a rainbow (literally). Many of my behaviors are learned, but we still have our own uniqueness. They are the reason why I have come to be who I am and very proud to say it too. We are not perfect, we argue, we fight, we even stop talking to each other at times; but in the end, we are family and our love will always be there. That's why we try and teach generation after generation after generation that no matter what, family is family!

If you can't already tell, my life as a youngster was pretty interesting. I won't get into all the family secrets, just my perception of what my life was like. Some things may be of surprise, but this is a tale of my legend (smile).

LIFE AS A YOUNGSTER

*Children are like wet cement, whatever falls
on them makes an impression.*

—Haim Ginott

As a youngster, my life was nothing ordinary. I had all these siblings, ten nephews (older and stairsteps behind me) and two nieces (just a little bit younger). My father and brother's first wives were first cousins (which no one could tell.) However, my brother knew my cousin before my mother met my father (just a coincidence, I think). This was a little weird growing up, but we just went with it. One thing is for sure, you can't help who you love!

My parents were thirty-eight (mom) and thirty (dad) when I was born, so I always had an ole soul, as they say. I didn't talk until I was about fourteen months old because I had my siblings to talk for me. So all I had to do was point to get what I wanted. My mom told me my dad asked her to ask the doctor why I wasn't talking at ten months, and the doctor told her, "Because she has siblings to speak for her." I was a very nifty child, I would say.

My mom said I would just cry and cry and cry, no matter what she would do, when I was a baby. My dad would even try to comfort me after he got off the night shift sometimes because he felt sorry for my mom. After a while, Sharon would come get me and sing to me, then I'd just stop crying and go to sleep (Sharon has a beautiful voice.) My mom could not figure out why I cried so much, but my sibling thought it was because she was too old having another child (laughing). However, once I stopped crying, I never cried again (unless watching TV shows [smiling]).

As a youngster, I can remember always being with Sharon. She would talk to me about everything which made me feel more relaxed with her. Sharon was more attached to me than my other siblings.

She treated me just like I was her child and sometimes getting upset when my parents wanted to take me. Sharon was like my second mom, but I could just talk to her about anything! I could talk to my mom about anything, but not like with Sharon, and it was probably because she talked to me about everything.

When I was five months, I had pneumonia and had to stay in the hospital for a week. After that one experience, I never got sick. It was a long stay, and I had to be confined to the crib until I was cured. My mom said, "You looked so sad just crawling up and down the crib." I couldn't stand to be confined!

When I started potty training, I remember my mom had to tie me to the pot (it was a wooden training pot with a plastic seat and a little compartment made like a bowl underneath to catch the waste which would sometimes come off) because I would not sit still. I would walk around with it and everything. The bottom falling out, I didn't care, I had things to do (presigns of ADHD, laughing). I just did not like to be confined to anything, plus I was claustrophobic. I couldn't stand tight places; I would get very nervous. I don't know if anyone ever knew that though (still a struggle today).

Sharon and a couple of my other siblings would always play hide-and-seek with me and tell me not to say anything for any reason, but when they would call my name, I would say, "Here I is!" They would get a kick out of me because I could never just keep quiet, no matter where they would try and hide me (giggling). I was even bribed by popcorn because I loved popcorn.

Sharon would always give my mom breaks from me by making me take naps, taking me with her to school, or just going with her where she went. She said when I went to school with her, I would just sit there with my book or paper and just sit quietly. The teachers and other kids loved me and would ask about me when I wasn't with her. If I did not go with her, I would watch *General Hospital* while I was sitting on the potty chair so I could tell her about Luke and Laura when she came home from school. That was our show, and she would tell me when I started school (our bonding time)! We did this for many years. Now we don't even watch it (giggling).

Sharon told me I feared dark-complexed individuals, dolls, being in the dark, and cotton candy. I wonder why I feared cotton candy? It was probably because someone told me a horror story about it (a sick sense of humor). I feared many things, and my family got a kick out of scaring me (smiling). However, I did not think it was funny, but that was humorous to them (shaking my head). Nowadays people would say that was child abuse (society changes). There was no harm done! We just had fun as children do!

I could remember people, places, and events like they happened yesterday. I never forgot a face or anything, for that matter! I was always aware of what was going on, even when they thought I didn't know. No, I wasn't prying, just very observant and inquisitive. I even knew directions when we traveled. I hardly forgot anything!

I was a child who basically tried to keep to myself, but growing up with all those nephews, that was not happening. They would just pick on me and pick on me until I got mad and had to earn my respect (whooping some butts). Yes, we wrestled and played, but I would never let them get the best of me. We would do everything together except bathe. They were the extension of my siblings in a way. I was the only girl, most of the time, which didn't bother me at all. I wasn't the prissy type anyway! Whatever my nephews did, I did too (almost I was a little smarter than them) until Marilyn came around, wanting to complain to Mommy I was acting like a boy (always in my business). My mom wouldn't say anything, though, because that's who I had to play with at the time.

With all this family and I being the only child to my father, you would think I was a complainer. Nope, I didn't complain at all—only if you invaded my space. I just milked the situation because my siblings were so much older than me, I got what I wanted for the most part. Although many of them had their own children, they always made time for me or to involve me in some capacity. I held a lot in, though, because I understood a lot.

Some of my siblings' families weren't what I thought they should have been, and most of the time, depending on which sibling, I would tell them about my concerns. The others I would just keep quiet because they wouldn't listen. I would tell my mom sometimes, though, if I felt there was danger, and she would get on them (she was the mother, I figured she could do something). I wasn't trying to be a snitch, but I just thought things could be better, and I knew they could do better, especially with their children. It was even more prevalent because most of them were not mistreated in any way by our parents.

I remember sleeping with my mom until I was a teenager because my dad worked at night. We would just talk about everything, and since she had so many children, we were her best friends. I went everywhere with her once Sharon moved away. My life was to please my mom and not being a disappointment for any reason (at five years old, I figured this out.)

I just took things as they came and dealt with it because there was nothing I could do anyway (stayed in a child's place). I grew up not allowed to be in grown-folk business (which that's how it should be), so my opinion did not mean anything. It actually helped me cope and gain leadership skills because I had to take care of my nephews and nieces when they were around. I was a child, though, no real responsibilities, just looking out for them! I did not grow up fast at all (the way it should be).

I did play football with the boys, though. I loved football! Yes, I was very much a tomboy. I was not a boy! I wanted to do everything the boys could do because girls' things were too prissy. I liked to climb trees, race the boys, run around outside, play football, play with toy cars and trucks, make pies out of dirt (good cooking [giggling]), break dance, and play with my nephews and neighborhood friends. It was mostly boys around me when I grew up anyway, so I really had no choice but to act a little like them.

There were two girls who lived across the street, but I only befriended the one, Lorie, who acted like a tomboy (funny). I remember my nephews making us physically fight, but I wouldn't fight her back because she was my friend, and friends didn't fight. She was a year older than me. I remember after that fight, my dad telling me I better never let anyone beat me in a fight, or I had to answer to him (scared). I didn't think it was a fight, though, but I just got mad and remembered what he said, so as you can see, I basically grew up with my nephews and got in trouble behind them too (shaking my head with a smirk).

I was very spoiled by everyone but very respectful. I got everything I wanted and more, never worrying about the price—I just wanted it (rotten to say the least). If one person didn't get it, someone else did. My grandmother, aunts (my mom's sisters), siblings, and in-laws really could have made me awful to the point I wasn't to be told no (I don't like to be told no though [smiling]), but it didn't. I do have lavish taste! I became more appreciative after my mom made me pick out my own things for Christmas one year (about thirteen years old), and that's all I got (not cool, not cool at all.) That is all I woke up to on Christmas that year! It was awful! That experience showed me that when you are not appreciative of when others are taking time out of their lives and spending their money on you, be grateful for whatever they do for you. They do not have to do anything for you if they don't want to! It only took one time for things to happen with me that would change my thinking forever. I made major adjustments based off one experience. I never thought erratically, but I did make changes that would benefit me in the future. During this experience, I learned that if I wanted something, I had to work for it once I got older. Whatever I wanted, I had to work for it! It made me more open-minded, but once my mind was made up, there was little change you could do. I was opinionated, though!

As a youngster, I never really considered myself as being a very friendly person, but everyone was always talking to me and telling me their problems (shaking my head). I could not figure it out, but I would just listen and sometimes would just say what made sense to me (from a child's point of view at least). They would sometimes listen, so it must have worked (smiling).

I was always inquisitive, creative, and analytical in any situation. Maybe that's why everyone wanted to talk to me about their lives (shrugging shoulders) In addition, I never told family, friends, or other people's business because I thought if they wanted you to know, they would tell you themselves (I'm still that way). This was very different than most of my family members because most of them ran their mouths about everyone else but wouldn't talk about what they were doing (shaking my head). That wasn't me!

As I was growing up with my nephew, they would always involve me in their situations. I was their backup, but I really wasn't because they would get caught without me having to get involved. The twelve of us were very close, different, but raised by my mom at some point. We had fun being kids and acting like kids with no worries. My mom protected all of us from whatever would harm us or cause a negative reaction. Some heeded to her words, but most did not, but that was a choice they made because a good foundation was laid for all of us, even if there were some tribulations. My mom is our *rock*!

I can remember having a few kids outside of my family that I called my friends: Lorie (neighborhood), Trini (school and church), and Bridgett (school). They would always confuse Bridgett and I, but we looked nothing alike (very confusing and frustrating). Lorie (August 1973) was not friends with Trini (April 1974) or Bridgett (July 1974) because she went to a different school and was my neighborhood friend. However, Trini and Bridgett were friends, and I was the baby of the group (funny). I brought them together, and I ended up being the youngest. This was one of the starts of my leadership qualities (smile).

As a youngster, I never felt I needed friends because I had such a large family. I always felt that girls were jealous, and the boys just wanted inappropriate things from me, which I would fight them before that would ever happen. I did know how to stick up for myself at a very early age (especially with hide-and-seek). When it came to things, I did not accept from anyone, I knew what measures to take in order to rectify the situation (mostly punching the crap out of you and meaning it—a little sadistic). I was never a follower, I did my own thing always (leadership quality)!

I even had two cousins my age that added to me not thinking I wanted friends: Carrie (November 1974) and Travaul (January 1975). We grew up in our family church at the Beulah Baptist Church, Smithfield, Pennsylvania where our Tracy ancestors basically built the church in the country in the late 1800s. There were other families who attended, but the Tracy family was more prevalent. When my mom started taking her family, then the Tracys and Pratts dominated, especially among the children of the church. So my cousin (Duke) affectionately started referring to us (Carrie, Travaul, Jeanine, and myself) as the big four because we were always together growing up. Jeanine is my eldest niece from my brother Mike. I had another cousin, Telsha, who was a year younger than Jeanine, but she wasn't as mature as we were at our age, I guess (honestly I never really asked why she wasn't included).

As you can tell, I was the oldest, of course (not an honor, not an honor at all), so any problem among us, I was always getting the flack for it (disappointing and nerve-racking). They were prissy and I was always the tough one out of the group (smiling). Although my family only bought me girl things, and I dressed in dresses a lot, I was tougher than them and didn't want to be seen as prissy at all. The only girly thing I wanted was my hair (giggling). I took pride in making sure my hair was always done and cute. Although looking at some of my pictures, whoa boy!

When I started school, my sister Sharon would always put me in a dress for some odd reason, and oh my, she did not like me to get dirty. She would change my clothes a thousand times if I got a little dirt on me (can we say obsessive-compulsive disorder, OCD [smiling]). She said little girls should never be dirty. Man, did she live by that!

As I got a little older, I wore shorts under my dresses. Remember I was a tomboy, so I played with the naughty boys (smirk). Boys just being boys, really! I always hated dresses, but as I said before, I had to have my hair girly! I remember in many of my school pictures, I had gone to school and redone my hair because I wanted it a certain way (my mom bought the pictures too [shake my head, smiling]). Oh boy, you never think, as a child, what you do will eventually catch up to you when you become an adult (giggling). My mom said there would be times like this! My do-it-yourself styles were not what I thought they would be (giggling). I have pictures to prove it!

I know I would have rather worn pants with a beautiful hairdo, but that wasn't girly (ugh). Girls wore dresses! However, when it was okay to wear pants, I think I was the first to wear them everywhere as a child. Don't get me wrong, when I played outside, I wore pants; but if we had to go places, I was usually in a dress of some sort (romper, skirt, dress, etc.). Most dresses were form-fitting, and I did not like to show my shape at all. Yes, I was very petite with a nice shape for my age, but I wanted it to stay hidden. The bigger the clothes, the better was my motto! I just wasn't the prissy type and didn't care how anyone felt about it. I enjoyed boy activities because I could relate better. It came in handy (smiling)!

My family bought me Barbie dolls (with all the accessories), doll babies, and all the latest girl toys. I would only play with them when my cousins or other girls came around, or I went to their houses. For the most part, they would stay in their boxes until I had girl company (not Lorie, though, because she was a tomboy too). One thing I know is I did not want anyone touching my toys, you had to play with your own. I didn't like girly toys, but I didn't want you wearing my toys out either (smiling). I think I was quite sadistic as a child when I think about it, huh.

I remember when Jeanine got a little older, she wanted to act like a tomboy, but Mike was not having it (smiling). She did play basketball like the boys, though. We were pretty close for the most part, but as we got older, she was closer to my cousins. It just seemed that I always stuck out because I did not do what everyone else was doing. Even my nephews and I grew apart. It felt like I went right, and everyone else around me went left (wondering). Except for my niece Shayna, we have similar characteristics (probably because of Sharon, though).

I do remember, I did not like black dolls or dark-complexioned people at all! The dolls were not the same complexion as myself, so I wanted white (peach) ones. I was just so disgusted that they represented the black dolls as actually being black. I knew about black face, but this was the '70s and '80s. Those characters and dolls did not exist now. I couldn't understand why we had to be so misunderstood because of our color (still an issue today). We were just all different shades of brown complexion, what was so hard about making our toys look like us? I would not play with a doll that was black (confused and angry). I would not accept it!

I learned at an early age about color and how black people were so misrepresented in such a white country (no disrespect to others). I wasn't taught to be racist, but my father and grandmother did not want me to be involved with any Caucasian boys. I could have them as my friends but nothing else. We had enough problems being black, and they did not want me to have to go through any other unnecessary problems. This was the start of my personal feelings about people and color. I knew if you looked a certain way and acted a certain way, you would get more accomplished, but behind your back, they were stealing our ideas. Not something a young curious child should grow up understanding because my perception of individuals would be forever altered (shaking my head).

Now I wouldn't go to dark-complexioned people, but I loved my grandfather on my father's side who was chocolate. My grandparents were just amazing to me! My grandfather stood 6'3", dark-complexioned black man, and my grandmother stood about 4'10", light-complexioned, almost-white mixed woman (she considered herself black). My grandmother did not like white people, and she was half-white (go figure). My grandfather never really showed color too much, only when he was high off the apple juice, and he talked about blond-hair blue-eyed white women in his sleep. I never knew what that was about, and my grandmother never said anything (skeptical).

I did ask my grandmother one day why she did not like white people, and her reply was, "I just don't trust them." And that was that (since she gave me this look of death if I asked any more questions about it). However, I was curious, so I did ask again and again and again but always got the same answer (very strange). She did not like to talk about her past, and I think it was because her mother left the family to move to live in Detroit, Michigan, and her father wouldn't let them see her. She has a bunch of pictures of her mother's family (who were her Caucasian family) but never talked about her. My grandmother just would not budge (stubborn)!

I learned about my grandfather's family at our yearly Tracy family reunions. Most of my grandfather's family were still living, so they could tell stories with much detail which made it easier for my cousins to find out about our ancestors. It would take years, but eventually, we got far enough where we knew most of who we were and where we originated from. Funny thing is that most of my grandfather's siblings were of dark complexion, and their children were dark. I did not go to most of them; I just stared mostly. I only liked individuals with my complexion or lighter, but not white (I was prejudiced, not honorably, though).

Now learning about my mom's parents and family would come later, but there really isn't much we can go on because my grandfather moved from down South to the North into the military and changed his name. So the research is still ongoing, but we do have family reunions every year, just with the immediate families on my mom and dad's side. My mom said her father never talked about it, and they never asked (more work for us). She said that they did not ask questions like we do because they didn't know to ask or think to ask, just went with whatever their parents told them. My grandfather was a mulatto, and my grandmother was black. He was twenty-five, and she was thirteen when they got married. He was born in Florence County in Sumter, South Carolina, to Wilbur Richardson and Olley Perkins, and they had six children. We think my grandfather's name was Julius Richardson and was born in 1892. Records are very hard to find from that time! My mom knew her mother's mom and dad, though. This is very intriguing and leads to many more questions and much research (a task I will quest later in my life.)

For some reason, I can remember a lot being revealed, or I better understood, when I became ten years old. My inquisitiveness kicked in, I guess, or my intellectual skills increased. It was something! I wondered why black people were so misrepresented because we were just different shades of brown, not black.

I learned about puberty (ah, they could have saved this one!). That's when relationship conversations started being asked or talked about (which I was nowhere near concerned about that). In fifth grade, the school taught us about puberty and womanhood. We had to watch a video and look at pictures of body parts of both sexes. I don't remember much because I spent most of my time trying to get out the room because I was feeling sick. I made up every excuse

I could to not have to participate in this life-changing experience. Although some of the people I hung around were already experiencing these things, I just knew it wasn't for me.

I began understanding my place in the family and life in general. I started having challenges, personally. I didn't quite understand why there were so many more whites who were in poverty than blacks, but we were the minority. This started more of my inquisitive thoughts concerning the world. My mom would talk to me about everything that she knew about when it came to color, diversity, or whatever I would want to talk about. My mom was always honest with us, no matter what we would ask, if she knew about it. If it was not age appropriate, she would just say we would talk about it later. I think by my mom allowing me to be so open, I just felt it was okay to be like that with everyone. If I wanted to know something, I would just ask. Like one time, I remember asking my aunt if she could see her feet because her breast was the biggest I had ever seen. She laughed and said, "Yes, I can see my feet!" Then proceeded to tell me that I just ask people anything (which I really did [nodding my head yes]). I just knew and wondered way too much at ten years old, but it just expanded the older I became. Funny thing is, my Caucasian friends used to ask me black questions too which made me even more curious.

I can remember around this age, my friends and family started wanting to experiment with adult behavior such as smoking cigarettes. I never tried it, but I was always the one preaching to them as to why they should not be doing it (leadership quality). I hated the smell of smoke, so I knew I would never try it, plus my lips and gums were already dark so why add to the misconception? I did not like having dark lips or gums, but I just worked it in my favor, not really allowing peers to clown me. I had a few but not too many peers who would say anything to me because I had a smart mouth, and they did not know what I would say back that would be hurtful (sinister).

Around this time was when I did get my first black doll. It was brown! I guess this was when I realized that a person's skin color bothered me. It was not intentional nor was it taught by a specific individual; it was just something my young mind picked up on very early in life. Unfortunately it really stuck after this and affected my actions and perceptions! I guess this is how children start to understand color which has not been taught but recognized by people's actions (the evil of this world). This was a downfall and uprise for many people of black descent. It all depended on where you lived, socioeconomic status, and character (slave mentality).

One of the most important actions I pursued was the love for taking naps. This was my way of coping and winding down (Sharon made me take naps, so I got used to them). They really came in handy, though, because I stayed out of trouble because I was napping when things were happening around me (smile). I was not an intrusive child, so if things were happening and I was napping, I did not get up to see what was happening unless it affected me in one way or the other. I thought way too much, and napping became a way in which I slowed my thinking down for a bit. I still take naps today, but it's more like just lying in silence because my children are running around.

I vaguely remember a lot about my elementary school years. I think when my brother got killed (Scott, shot in the head), I lost most of my childhood memories. Maybe that's why I remember the age of ten so well (my brother was killed when I was eight, turning nine). Maybe I didn't think elementary school was very important. I don't know (shrugging my shoulders)! What I do remember about it is in bits and pieces, and most of it doesn't even go together (distorted memory recognition).

I do recall fifth grade (ten years old) and up for some odd reason. I don't really remember my teachers, but I do remember things that happened and wondering where I fit in during this era of young life. I guess I just wanted to be me, and that was it and all! I didn't need to fit in because I never did. I always thought as a leader, not following anyone.

I do remember when I did start school, I was very shy and very observant. The other children gave me a hard time, but I never worried about them because I kept to myself, unless you talked to me. Whatever they were trying to give me a hard time about, I just would turn the attention back on them, and they would leave me alone (a way with words, I guess). I felt that they weren't part of my existence, so their opinions of me never really mattered (egocentric maybe). I had a big family, so what did I care about other children's opinions of me? It did make me have tougher skin, though, because kids said some cruel things, but I just would sit there and not say a word until they said something about my family, and I'd speak up defensively. It wasn't until I got in middle school that I started speaking up on all types of situations where others were being mistreated. I did not like for you to think you had power or control over what others could do or say, so I would stick up for them no matter what the outcome.

Fortunately I never got into trouble, and I kept good grades. I was always in the principal's office helping when I did not want to be bothered with anyone. They allowed me to file papers or whatever I could do because I was a good student and liked having something to do to stay out of trouble. I guess that's when I understood the phrase "brownnose." I wasn't but the bad kids didn't need to know that because they couldn't do anything to me. I had a very smart mouth when it came to kids, though, and I never backed down, ever! They would try me for a minute, then once I'd say what I had to say, the conversation would end, unless there was a troublemaker in the crowd. It never escalated to anything physical, just talk. I probably would have gotten in trouble then because I did not like anyone putting their hands on me. However, once I got in middle school, girls started not liking me because of how I looked or the boys liking me or whatever their immature emotions were feeling. Those are the times I did feel I was going to have to fight because I'd let you talk, but as soon as you thought about threatening me, I was a different person. Then I would think, *I'm not even mentally or psychologically where they are with maturity, so why am I getting myself worked up for nonsense? They want to be bothered with grown folks' actions, let them be because I want no parts of it. I have a bright future ahead and worrying about puberty issues, no thank you!*

My low self-esteem started around this time too because I was advanced in some subjects but struggled with reading because I could not read out loud. Back then, they went around the room calling on you to read the lesson out loud to the class, and I was so, so nervous because I knew I would stumble over my words, even though I had a rich vocabulary. This was also when I remember them placing all black and low-income white children in what we called special math and reading classes. I was very good at math, so I really don't know why I was in that class; but as I said, they just automatically placed the black kind-of-bright students in these classes. It just helped us develop stronger skills!

I was just very scared to read in front of people because I was shy, and I never liked to be wrong. I understood what I read when I read to myself, but I was just reading words when I read out loud, not comprehending anything. This was a disadvantage for me because my mom always said, "If you don't want black people to know something, just write it down." Every time I would read out loud, I would think about her saying that, but it did not help my reading comprehension out loud, just when I read to myself.

I remember Marcia telling my mom, "Mommy, LaShawn's reading is atrocious!" because I was in her Sunday school class, and I read very slow for a ten-year-old. When my mom got wind of that, oh my goodness, I had to start reading everything from the newspaper, magazines, books, the Bible, or anything written down (oh, I was so mad at Marcia). I was reading out loud in no time, though, and comprehending (somewhat). I used to wish Marcia never said anything, but it helped me, so I guess I should thank her (smiling while rolling my eyes). However, I still struggle a little reading out loud, but I figured out if I read it to myself first, then I won't scuffle. I am a trainer too (eyes wide open)!

I remember in fifth grade, these boys were doing something they were not supposed to do, and I was sitting, watching them, but not really concerned with what they were doing because it was none of my business. Well, when we grew up, you were permitted to be paddled by your teachers if you misbehaved, then again by neighbors, older siblings, and eventually when you got home. So they lined up about five boys on the wall and was ready to paddle them, and I guess no one would talk, so they called me to tell them what happened. Was that a mistake? I didn't say anything (steadily twisting my ponytails). They called my mom to go to the school to see if I would talk, and I said nothing. She told them, "She's not going to talk" (while shaking her head no). The boys all thought I talked, but I didn't. They all got paddled that day. I was scared out of my mind because I minded my own business when it wasn't pertaining to me, so why would the teachers try to get me involved (smiling)? I'm not a snitch, and that's just my personality—to keep to myself!

From the time I was ten years old, I stressed I did not want children. I knew I wasn't a nurturer, nor very affectionate, and that wasn't something I wanted to grow into either. I had plans, and I did not want to deal with a child. No, not never (selfish a little)! I had seen my siblings struggling, and I did not want that feeling at all. Plus I was always watching my siblings' children (which I hated but liked because I could get paid). I enjoyed them when they were babies, but once they started talking, I didn't want to babysit anymore nor change diapers. It was time to quit, and the money wasn't that good for all that work!

Once I became a teenager, things started to change in my life. I knew I had things I wanted to do, and I needed my priorities in order for them to come true. I became very focused in life and the choices that I made. My mom sat at the kitchen table, and we would talk about everything. Her conversations helped me deal with a lot of different adolescent issues and concerns. That's why I wasn't concerned with having a relationship with a boy because they were just a distraction. I wasn't even really interested in having or making friends either. My small circle of friends was fine with me because the more people you let into your life, the more problems that come along with them. I watched how people manipulated individuals to get what they wanted, and I hated it. Once I got that feeling, I did not think there was any boy on my level, so I was not going to be manipulated by what others felt I should be doing. Unfortunately I was really picked on about it and called names which, in turn, made me want a relationship to shut them up. I did not want anything serious, just a friendly relationship! I had plans, and a boy was not in it. However, when I turned about fifteen, I got a boyfriend just to shut people up, but that was a big mistake because it was all a game. When

I found out, I just went back to just being acquaintance with boys. I will talk more about my courtships later.

My senior year, things changed when I met Michael. The wanting to date, a serious relationship, a boy in my plans—it all changed. There was something about him that made things different. He was a challenge for me, even though he was younger than me. This was when my thoughts became cloudy but focused. I still had my dreams and plans, it was just slightly altered. He just had to graduate from high school first, and we needed to grow up more before anything really serious could happen. There will be more details in the courtship chapter.

I basically went with the flow when I wanted to. I was always a leader, never a follower. I do know that I stressed to everyone that I never wanted to have children or get married. I took every precaution to make sure this never happened. Plus my mom told me, "Every person you have sex with, you better make sure that person is good enough to be the father of your children," which terrified me even more, so having sexual acts was not a priority of mine. I had plans and wanted to achieve them with no interruptions. Boys thought that I was a challenge, so they would make bets to see who could get with me first (shake my head); so immature. It did not interest me!

Since our family was already growing, I did not wish to add to it. I just wanted to graduate and go to college. I would fill in the blanks as I went along if I needed to, but I wanted my PhD degree by the time I was thirty-five years old. I didn't know in what concentration, but I knew that I wanted to be able to conduct practical research. I did not want to be like my brothers and sisters, having babies, in bad relationships, not graduating from college, or even not going to college. I loved to learn, and that's all I could really think about as a youngster growing up.

Early on, my mom thought I was going to be a doctor because I was intrigued about babies being born. Since I loved to learn, that would not have been a problem. However, after I started really learning about it and not having a stomach for blood, slobber, vomit, or traumatic experiences, she knew that was not going to be my profession. After my brother's death, my whole life changed, and it played a major role on my perception. I developed fears that I never experienced before which took part of my innocence as a child. I knew my career had to be something I could manage myself (entrepreneurship/business owner). I did not want to work for someone else. I had to be my own *boss*! This led to me understanding the real-life variations of family and how these factors affected some of my outcomes.

REAL-LIFE VARIATIONS OF FAMILY

You don't choose your family. They are God's gift to you, as you are to them.

—Desmond Tutu

I lived my life by experiences of mine or from my family. When you are the youngest of a big family (eleven siblings, forty-nine nieces and nephews, and fifty-six great-nieces and nephews), certainly there are things that are expected (these great-nieces' and nephews' numbers are much larger now and growing). Mine was no different! My family pushed me to be better than some of them and (to me) lived their life through me. I was a very respectful child who never really, really challenged what my family told me (a born leader). I had my own mind, but they had a big influence over me that sometimes clouded my judgment as to who I really was. It wasn't intentional, but I was just that impressionable. I love my family and put them first.

My siblings have never treated me any different than being their little sister. We were raised as one, even though my siblings had their father around until November 1998. He never treated me any different either. When he would come get my sisters, I would tag along as well (smiling). My nickname for him was The Bandit, off the Clint Eastwood TV show *Smokey and the Bandit*, with the little orangutan (laughing) because I was always getting in the car when he picked up my sisters like I belonged (giggling). In my eyes, I did belong! We were all one big happy family.

My mom was thirty-eight, about to be thirty-nine, and my father was thirty when I was born. So pretty much, I was born with an ole soul. My parents had different interest when I was growing up except they both were Christians. My mom served on many boards and in many organizations, sometimes being the only black, but she was well respected, dedicated, and devoted to helping others (helping blacks find jobs in Fayette County, Pennsylvania). She worked full-time at the Fayette County courthouse as a tax assessor most of my upbringing, went back to college to receive her bachelor's degree in business management, graduating in 1985, raised some of my nephews and myself, and was a wife. My dad worked in the coal mines in Clarksville, Pennsylvania, as a supervisor, mostly working the night shift. He is an undiagnosed alcoholic (although he would disagree), but he never missed out on family events or work. He wrecked every car we had because of his drinking, but he never was hurt or hurt anyone else (God looking out for fools). He lived with us, but he never treated me any different from the rest of my family, unless he was drinking, then he wanted to talk to me (go figure). It bothered me that I wasn't Daddy's little girl, but in his own way, I guess, he did treat me a little different (silent struggle). I would get upset when he wouldn't come to some of my activities because he was drinking, but that's just who he was, and I had to understand he had a problem (he will never admit it). I love both my parents with their flaws and would not have changed them from being the parents God selected for me. I speak about my family's flaws because it will help you understand the importance behind me protecting my children later in my story.

As the stories are told to me, my siblings did not want another sibling because they thought my mom was "too old," and most of them were grown or teenagers. They told me they would have rather had a horse (laughing). Joan would just pick on me because I took her place after ten years. At one point, my mom told me she wasn't my mom, but my dad was my dad, that's why I didn't look like her. I was a little bothered, but that's the kind of sense of humor we have (strange to some).

We are a family with very strong opinions, temperaments, personalities, dispositions, and show little emotion. The men in the family are spoiled and self-centered (selfless at times), and the women are very strong and independent. However, we love one another, just as they are. The men are more emotional than the women. I grew to understand this at a very early age (smile). Some may call us dysfunctional, but we understand each other, and that's all that counts.

We stick together no matter what, and that's how we were taught. The women are more aggressive, though! We weren't allowed to fight among ourselves but don't mess with us. My mom made that clear very early that we were family and not to let anyone come between us no matter what (right or wrong). She taught it to the grandchildren as well which she was very close to all of them (twelve grandchildren who grew up with me at the time).

My siblings talked to me a lot when I was younger, especially Sharon, Marilyn, Duane, and Scott (deceased). Sharon and Scott would take me everywhere with them like I was their child. They were the ones who took me to get my ears pierced when I was five months (no, they didn't give my parents the chance). I remember always being with Sharon the most, even after she had her own daughter, Shayna, in November 1980. Which you can guess, I did not like Shayna because she was taking my place (hurt). But Sharon wasn't my mom, so I shouldn't have even been mad. I was, though! Everywhere Sharon lived, I would always go visit and sometimes stay for a little while. We have a special bond!

Shayna and I were more like sisters than niece and aunt. Marilyn's son, Patrick (1977), was my brother/nephew as they called us because he was raised with me. They used to dress me and Jeanine (Mike's daughter) the same for whatever reason (I hated it), but I guess because her mom, Roxanne, and Sharon were best friends, it made sense somehow. These are memories that stick out the most to me because it was strange, but we worked it out.

I can remember them making Jeanine and I dance and sing in front of them. We knew all the latest dances, so we performed for whoever was in the room when they called us at the time. We had a good time! I was even break-dancing and spinning on my head (laughing) since those were the dances in the early '80s. I stopped dancing, though, after I got into an altercation in a club over this man putting his hands up my skirt and getting kicked out. After that, dancing wasn't fun anymore (sad).

I loved to play football (quarterback) with my nephews. It seemed like I had a gift for it or something but could only play at home because that wasn't a girl's sport. I played football until I was about fourteen years old. The naughty boys would want to come up on our hill and play because they thought they could be naughty with me, but that was so short-lived. I would fight (literally punch the crap out of you) if you would try and touch me or tackle me for no reason. I was rough, but you were always warned (smile)!

I can remember when we would go on trips or to church, there would be like eight to ten children piled up in the car. I would always be in the front, though, because I was the girl. The boys would be in the back on laps, the floor; however, we needed to fit to get to where we were going. See, back then, seat belts were not the law. We could travel anywhere without seat belts and did not worry about accidents because those cars were so heavy, if you hit someone, you would just put a dent in it (well, our cars at least). For there to have been so many of us, we did not do a lot of arguing as kids. We just really enjoyed each other's company, I guess. I was really the only moody one because I would get tired of them and go to my room to take a nap (laughing). Oh, how I loved a good nap!

So as you can see, I was raised with my nieces and nephews (all twelve of them). I have two older nephews, and the others are stair-steps behind me (literally). Fortunately there are none my age, but they are right behind me (interesting). That's what happens when you are the youngest of twelve children and your mom has her first child at fifteen years old.

It was difficult sometimes, but I earned my respect from all of them (smiling). My mom would not have had it any other way because she believed in family, although her mom passed away when she was only six years old, and she had to help raise her sisters and help her daddy. She raised us to the best of her ability without having a mother to really show her how to be the best mother possible; she did a marvelous job on the entire family.

When I was growing up, a few of my brothers were very abusive to their wives or girlfriends, and I hated it (physically and mentally). My sisters were even abused by their husbands or boyfriends, and that just was not right on so many levels. They would fight back, though, but a woman cannot beat a man no matter how strong she is! This was a struggle for me because I just couldn't understand. Interesting, though, that my mom was mentally abusive to my father who did his dirt but never put his hands on her or mentally abused her. I believe my mom wasn't going to take another man trying to control her, so she made things clear very early.

As I was growing up, I observed these actions and made a promise to myself that this would never happen to me, and I meant it. If you feel you need to talk down to me or put your hands on me, then there is no need for this relationship to continue. I did get into one relationship were things went left instead of right, but I justified that very quickly and left that situation where it was, never turning back. I knew then that I would never get in a relationship where a boy/man put his hands on me or vice versa, not even talking to me—crazy wasn't allowed. I had one father, and he never put his hands on me or talked to me crazy so a boy/man could never try it! That was a cold case ready to happen because it would have been premeditated on my end (seriously). I would not tolerate that at all, and since my mom was abused by her first husband, and I learned the stories, I was too strong for that to happen to me without you getting killed. I don't play that!

When things would happen, as I said before, I took a nap. However, once I got to high school, someone would interrupt my nap mostly for nonsense. I had a serious attitude when my naps were interrupted, and it wasn't pretty for anyone. A nap just made me feel refreshed, and the interruption was just devastating! I needed my naps! Whatever was wrong could have waited, and I would have dealt with it once I was reinvigorated. Funny, though, my naps weren't your average naps. I went to sleep for about two hours and would still go to bed at night! I just love to sleep, it's one of my hobbies. Unfortunately my mind never sleeps (that's probably why I love naps), and it has given me insomnia the older I get.

One thing I really hated was talking on the phone. I wasn't a talker, so the conversations would, most of the time, be one-sided, and I had made my own phone restrictions. You couldn't call me before 9:00 a.m. on Saturdays (it may have been noon by the time I was a senior) and after 9:00 p.m. anytime. I remember a few times staying on the phone with the boy I dated in tenth grade, but it was more breathing than anything else, and it was so annoying to me. I would talk to you when I see you, and that was enough for me. That was for everyone, even family! I would rather spend time together rather than talk on the phone with nothing to talk about.

I only spent time with Michael mostly at his house because I did not like anyone coming to my house. Since dating wasn't a big thing with me, I didn't have a problem not having males over. Plus my nephews were always into stuff, so I did not need my business in the street with them! I only dated two boys in high school, but Michael was truly my best friend. He may have been two years younger than I, but we really understood each other. It could have been we were both raised by an older generation.

As I previously stated, I went with the flow, but being promiscuous was not of interest to me. Since children nor marriage were not in my future dreams, I couldn't afford a slipup. I just had to keep my body safe because I just knew a child would ruin any plans I had for a future, and I had already seen my family struggle, and that was not for the kid (shaking my head).

I can't remember the "talk" much with my mom, just that she told me that family planning was down the street, and if I was thinking about it, that I needed to go there to get protection (real talk). I guess she had so many talks that once I came along, she just told me basically to be safe since she knew I did not want children. She says she gave me a book to read (I don't remember a book)! On the other hand, my sisters gave me the real scenario (eyes wide open). Basically terrifying me from even wanting to be touched by the opposite sex (laughing).

In fifth grade, the school taught us about puberty and womanhood. We had to watch a video and look at pictures of body parts of both sexes. I don't remember much because I spent most of my time out of class, as I stated previously. Unfortunately I did not need much of the talk anyways because I was fifteen years old, turning sixteen, when I became a woman. During that time, I was considered old (smiling). My sisters and brothers had been schooling me for so long I thought I was a pro at knowing what to do (laughing). Little did I know, there was much more I needed to know (eye opener). Some of the people I hung around with were already having sex and babies (shocking). It wasn't for me because I had plans, I always had plans!

I tried to get my tubes tied at eighteen years old, and I was serious as a heart attack. The doctor laughed, but I was so serious. In 1992, the FDA came out with the Depo-Provera which was a shot you got in your buttock or fatty part of your upper arm in the doctor's office that lasted for three months. I jumped at this, oh how I jumped! I would go every three months like clockwork. They would say you needed to come off it for a little while a few years later, but I wasn't worried about any side effects. I started in December of 1992 until November 1997, because of my moving to a different state, and I did not have a doctor. Truth be told, my sister-in-law would send it to me when I first moved for about three months until I could get insurance and go to the doctor's. So I had to stop and wait for my menstrual cycle to start before the doctor could start administering it again. I started back in January 1998, and continued until December 2002. This was when I tried birth control pills which was a disaster for me (sad)! I was on the Depo-Provera for approximately nine years, and I had no side effects at all. I named it the child-free shot. I loved it! In addition, there was no menstrual cycle, I was ecstatic! I also used protection as well because it did not stop other diseases!

I just wanted to go to college and become successful without having to worry about anyone but myself (selfish). I watched my siblings and my mom struggle, so I just wanted to live freely and enjoy life. My ultimate goal was to travel with whatever career I chose. I always focused and did not need a distraction.

My family played a major role in my life, and it shows in all facets of my life. I love them no matter what our flaws. They don't really understand me, but it's all right because I like it like that most of the time.

As a child and teenager, I can remember us being a traveling family! We would travel to any state my siblings resided, plus the Tracy family reunions were in different states every year, along the East Coast. I remember visiting Erie, Pennsylvania; Cleveland, Akron, Cincinnati, Columbus, Maple Heights, Garfield Heights, all in Ohio; Detroit, Michigan; New Britain, Connecticut; Philadelphia, Pennsylvania; Frederick, Maryland; Washington, DC; Virginia; New York; New Jersey; the Southern states when we drove to Disney World.

Our church took us to amusement parks every summer, usually in Pennsylvania, Ohio, or Virginia. When I was in ninth grade, my cousin Duke started taking us to visit all black colleges from Pennsylvania to North Carolina, giving us exposure to HBCU (Historically Black Colleges and Universities) campus life. I loved to travel! Since I had been to so many places before I graduated from high school, it wasn't hard when I selected two Southern HBCUs to attend that focused on electrical engineering which was Clark University and North Carolina A & T. I did not attend either school, but I'll explain later.

Something that sticks out for me when I was growing up was the amount of respect we had for adults and peers, even if things did go wrong for a while. We knew how to talk about things (positive or negative). Those were the days! As I matured into adulthood, I began to understand why we were taught those early morals, values, and respect.

LIVING WITH GLAUCOMA

I am always at my best when I am pushed against the wall.

—Unknown

On August 19, 1995, I was diagnosed with acute glaucoma. I first found out on a routine eye exam at the Uniontown Walmart in Pennsylvania where I always went to get my glasses (I have been wearing glasses since seventh grade). Now I always suffered migraines, but I never let it stop me. During my exam, they had this machine that blew a puff in your eye to determine the pressure of your optic nerve. Well, mine was 35 and 55 which was very high for a nineteen-year-old. So he checked it again with a tonometer (my eye was numbed), this blue light that actually touches your eyeball which would give a more accurate reading, but it was still the same. He had me come back in two weeks because I may have just been nervous which would increase the pressure. It didn't change! I believe it was higher than the first exam. So he sent me to Morgantown, West Virginia, to an ophthalmologist for further examination. There was where they diagnosed me with acute glaucoma in both eyes and recommended me to go to Dr. Gallo in Uniontown, Pennsylvania, which was closer to where I lived.

According to the glaucoma foundation (2015):

> Glaucoma is a group of eye diseases which in most cases produce increased pressure within the eye. This elevated pressure is caused by a backup of fluid in the eye. Over time, it causes damage to the optic nerve. Through early detection, diagnosis and treatment, you and your doctor can help to preserve your vision.

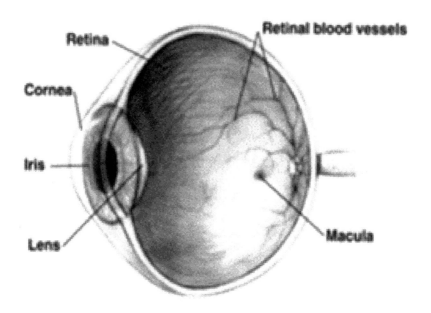

Normal Eye Image

Think of your eye as a sink, in which the faucet is always running, and the drain is always open. The aqueous humor is constantly circulating through the anterior chamber. It is produced by a tiny gland, called the ciliary body, situated behind the iris. It flows between the iris and the lens and, after nourishing the cornea and lens, flows out through a very tiny spongy tissue, only one-fiftieth of an inch wide, and called the trabecular meshwork, which serves as the drain of the eye. The trabecular meshwork is situated in the angle where the iris and cornea meet. When this drain becomes clogged, aqueous cannot leave the eye as fast as it is produced, causing the fluid to back up. But since the eye is a closed compartment, your "sink" doesn't overflow; instead the backed-up fluid causes increased pressure to build up within the eye. We call this open (wide) angle glaucoma.

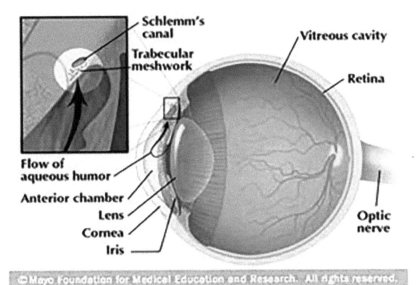

Aqueous humor continuously circulates from behind the iris into the anterior chamber. It exits the eye where the iris and the cornea meet. The fluid filters through the trabecular meshwork before passing into an open channel called Schlemm's canal.

Acute Glaucoma Image

To understand how this increased pressure affects the eye, think of your eye as a balloon. When too much air is blown into the balloon, the pressure builds, causing it to pop. But the eye is too strong to pop. Instead, it gives at the weakest point, which is the site in the sclera at which the optic nerve leaves the eye.

The optic nerve is part of the central nervous system and carries visual information from the eye to the brain. This cranial nerve is made up of over one million nerve axons, which are nerve fiber extensions of the retinal ganglion cells. When the eye pressure is increased and/or other inciting factors exist, the optic nerve becomes damaged and the retinal ganglion cells undergo a slow process of cell death termed "apoptosis." The death of the retinal cells and degeneration of the nerve fibers results in

permanent vision loss. Early diagnosis and treat-
ment of glaucoma can help prevent blindness.

When I was diagnosed, my optic nerve was the largest that they had seen in a person of my age or ethnic group (they still say that today when I go to the ophthalmologist). Glaucoma is genetic on your paternal side or from a sibling who might have it, most likely found in older black people. Since I did not know, at the time, of anyone on my father's side who said they were treating it, I couldn't figure out how I got it at such a young age. The doctor even said I could have been born with it, but it didn't flare up until I became older. After my diagnosis, my grandfather and father were diagnosed (ironic, huh).

This took me into a deep depression (stress moment). I had to take a semester off from college (fall of 1995) because I knew I would not be focused, so I worked instead and also taught myself how to cook with the help of *The Betty Crocker Cookbook*. My first meal I tried was sloppy joes. Now what made me think I could make sloppy joes from scratch, I don't know (giggling). My father is a picky eater, so he wouldn't eat my cooking. This was when I found out I had a heavy hand when it came to spices because those sloppy joes were so, so salty. My mother is an excellent cook, but she never taught us how to cook. She came home and tried to fix them, but I had too much salt. So that was my crash course in making sure I followed the directions.

Now I could cook homemade french fries, which I perfected! I picked that up from my father because he loves fried foods. But this teaching myself to cook was truly going to be a challenge, but I needed to take some of the stress of my mom since she worked so hard. Eventually I got it, and I made my mom and myself proud. I could *cook*!

Since I had no idea what was in store for me with this glaucoma, I just tried to stay busy. I knew I did not want to go blind, so I took the eye drops (Timoptic XE) which was a beta-blocker that would manage my pressure. It was later changed to Xalatan and Lumigan, all approved by the FDA. They could only get my control intraocular pressure (IOP) to 21 and 22 when it should be 10 to 12, but since my optic nerve was so thick, I would be okay and not need surgery.

I knew I would not be able to survive if I could not see because I thought it was the bane of my existence. It would just be devastating! I needed my eyesight; how can I relate to others if I couldn't see them? I use my eyes more than my words (observer). Then I realized, God's got this, and as long as I followed the doctor's treatment plan, I was going to be just fine. This was an illness, but I never looked at it that way because it was something no one could see. My first diagnosed illness (genetic)!

Glaucoma is a disorder of the eyes, as you have read, but it's not life-threatening unless you do not do what you are supposed to do. Please make sure you get regular eye exams for early detection. It has not stopped me in any way, shape, or form. I stay cautious, though! However, I have noticed that the older I become, the more I will have to take notice because I can get cataracts at an early age if not cared for properly. I just have put it in my God's hands, and I know that the devil is a lie if I am going to let this disorder get the best of me! Therefore, I had to find my place in a youth's world, knowing I have challenges with my eyes.

FINDING A PLACE IN A YOUTH'S WORLD

The inward journey is about finding your own fullness something that no one else can take away.

—Deepak Chopra

I was always focused when I was young, especially my teenage years. I knew what I wanted and what I needed to do to get it. I liked school because I knew an education could take me far in life. I was an A and B student most of my schooling until I got to seventh, ninth, and tenth grades. This was the time I knew education was not going to be easy if I wanted to continue to college and beyond. The adjustment and life's struggle being a teenager had a major influence on me during these times. But that was not long-lived because I just needed to challenge myself more. I wanted to be smarter than the white boys! Where I came from, they were always the smartest and excelled the fastest, so if I was as smart or smarter than them, I would be great. It wasn't what they called peer pressure; it was life! I never understood peer pressure, as they called it, until I became a teenager. I still did not fully understand it then. However, when the kids called me names and made fun of me, I thought it was because I was quiet, pretty, and smart (so they thought). I never acted like I was better than anyone, I just knew I had to study to get good grades. If that meant I could not hang with you, then so be it. You were not going to talk me out of my future goals and dreams.

At first, I would brush it off if the kids said something to me (it was boys who liked me and girls who were just jealous) until I got in seventh/eighth grade, and that's when I started speak up for myself. I learned early that they would pick on me because I was quiet, pretty, and smart (dumb reasons, though). But I had very low self-esteem that no one ever knew about. I carried a lot on my shoulders at a young age and never talked about it. So low self-esteem can kill an individual's spirit, but somehow, I did not let it affect me in such a manner (can't explain). Family situations were family secrets that you could not talk about, so I just kept it to myself and learned how to suppress it. This started my low self-esteem. I was the best at keeping secrets! Since I was quiet, you couldn't tell anyway. I never displayed anger for it, though, but my facial expression said differently (laughing). I understand that all families have some type of secrets, but it really doesn't help when you get older because there are things some should have learned so they do not repeat history. Some of my low self-esteem came from embarrassment too which I just started understanding (which is not really low self-esteem). Family issues are not necessarily your issues, but in most black families, we are taught that they are all our issues in one way or the other (confusing but understandable).

Once I became a teenager, I was so much more focused. I was told I walked around looking mean. I wasn't, though! I just didn't have time for foolishness, drama, or had a high tolerance for nonsense. I was just not interested and didn't really have time for teenage drama stuff. That's why I didn't know girls were getting pregnant in high school and having babies, or even having sex at some point. I was oblivious to those things because it did not affect me or concern me at this stage in my life. I had to worry about me, and my mom would have killed me if I even thought about getting pregnant or having sex at a young age. To my surprise, some people were having sex as early as twelve years old. What could you have possibly known at twelve? I just wanted to be a kid!

I was a nerd, you might say! I just knew there were things and places I wanted to go, and without an education, I couldn't get there (clever thinking). Don't get me wrong, I did enjoy life outside of school, it just wasn't a major priority in my young life. In my mind, belonging was never my strong suit (smile)! I knew I wanted to go to college, and the only way I would get there was to have good grades, not to get into any trouble, and limited hanging out with my so-called friends and family. This was when I noticed the split in my circle of family and friends. I had to think about and focus on my future because my mom was counting on me to do something with my life. In Fayette County, racism was very high, and I could not be very successful as an educated black woman there. To be very honest, I did not want to stay there anyway because there was no real wealth I could gain, and I was just more advanced than Fayette County. Racism would have killed my spirit or made me aggressive.

Unfortunately this got to my nephews, and they took a different way to be successful. They were so used to getting what they wanted they didn't want to work hard for it. I'll be the first to say that my brothers weren't the best role models then either. However, they knew right from wrong, and everyone worked hard for what they had in life. Some of my nephews just had to have fast money that cost them in the long run. That just wasn't smart at all to me! I was taught to be independent and to work hard for what I wanted. If it was given to me, I would have to basically sell my soul. I was too clever for that to happen. My soul was for me and wasn't for sale! I was not going to be manipulated by anyone for the sake of my well-being. I was taught to respect myself, and others would have no choice but to do the same. If not, then I was to move on. I was going to get ahead with my intellect, honesty, and work ethics. I wasn't going to let no one change that!

This was about the period when I started coming out of my shell (just a little) because teenagers would say inappropriate things, make fun of my family, especially my dad and brothers; and one time, they tried to talk about my mom having so many children, and I had to set them straight. I did not like people picking on others, and I would stand up for them and myself. I would do my research on the kids and use that as bait for my get backs (joaning today), if needed (smiling). Oh yeah, kids would talk about what was going to happen to me when I got older to try and kill my spirit! They said it because I wasn't interested in boys or doing things that would eventually get me in trouble. I respected my mom too much to let kids change me or get in my head with their nonsense of being teenagers. I had too much going for myself to fall into the teenage trap, even though my low self-esteem still existed. I just covered it up very well, I guess!

In tenth grade, I started going out with this boy, but I wouldn't let him distract me from what I wanted to do. I only did it because kids said I was gay! So I guess they did get to me a little (smile). It was more like puppy love after about a year! I thought it was love at the time, though. I was in tenth grade, and I didn't know what love really was when it came to the opposite sex because I did not need the headache and never really asked what it felt like. But when I found out he was sneaking around and getting girls pregnant, that put a very bad taste in my mouth about boys. I was pretty much done with worrying about having a boyfriend or falling in love with the opposite sex. We did hang out off and on until I finally cut it off at the beginning of my senior year. I really had to be focused on my books, and a boy was a distraction, especially when he wasn't right for me and on the same level as I was on. I couldn't afford being bothered with someone who did not have goals because I had dreams and a future to think about. I found out he was part of that fast life, and I was not interested in that movement at all (disappointed). There was never any room for an affectionate relationship in my future anyway. I had to be selfish with my time because I had success to achieve by a certain age! That kept me focused!

During this time, I also started driving (sixteen years old). My cousins and Jeanine would call me to go to the mall to hang out, but that wasn't something I was really into. I would go, but I did not like staying long. I got bored very fast! There I went again, standing out but not on purpose. I just always had a plan, and I guess during my teenage years, I really wasn't concerned with others. I thought they just couldn't do anything for me if we had nothing in common. In addition, I was too young for anything serious, but Carrie, Travaul, and Jeanine thought differently. Bridgett and Trini grew closer during this time, and it really became just me being me. I did not want to belong to a group or a set of friends, I just wanted to be left alone, really. I talked to who I wanted and did not care what others thought, period! I can honestly say that I had compassion for those I thought were different or misunderstood because I really was, if you think about it.

In high school, I had drama at school and at home, but I kept a level head. My grades did suffer in tenth grade because I took Algebra 3 and geometry which are not maths that should be taken together along with personal issues. I got my grades in these classes up before the end of the year, but it took a lot of studying and focusing. Every year after that, I took two math classes because I wanted to be an electrical engineer or own my own cosmetology shop with fashion, such as clothing and accessories. In 1990, Carrie and I attended Pitt University, Pittsburgh, Pennsylvania, for the summer for black children who were thinking about a career in engineering. It was a two-week program, and we stayed on campus. This was my first college-life experience! Carrie and I shared a room. We learned about all the different engineering degrees and which one would be most effective when we graduated from college. I believe we went two summers in a row (tenth and eleventh grades). We had the opportunity to meet children from Pittsburgh, Pennsylvania; Philadelphia, Pennsylvania; North Carolina; Richmond, Virginia; Florida; New York; but mainly children from the East Coast who were just as interested as we were in math and science field. I think Carrie only went because I was going (smiling.) It was a great learning experience and helped me decide on what I wanted to be when I grew up. After our eleventh grade year, they stopped the program, though. It was a great program which opened my eyes to other opportunities and careers I could seek. These types of programs were not offered to blacks as much as whites, so when I got the opportunity, I would jump at it. I always thought programs like these were great because black children could be exposed to the different career options if they were looking to go to college. My strongest subjects were math and science which were perfect for becoming an engineer. I was very, very interested! I struggled with economics and English (literature) classes throughout school.

Yes, I did most things teenagers did, if you were thinking otherwise! I went to school dances, and I was asked to the prom in ninth grade by one of the most popular seniors, but I turned it down because I wanted to wait for mine. In addition, I didn't really know why he wanted to go with a freshman anyway, but I was attractive when I dressed up (ego tripping.) Anyway I knew my parents weren't going for it! I also attended sporting events, played basketball from seventh until tenth grade (statistician for the boys and girls games when I retired), took tap dancing lessons from eight until fourteen years old, gymnastics and acrobatics from nine until eleven years old, played baseball for midget league at Bailey Park in Pennsylvania. I took ballet but only for a few months because I didn't like it, hung out at the mall (really didn't like to), and stayed in a teenager's place, not trying to grow up too fast.

I was very moody during my teenage years, especially at the end of tenth, going into eleventh, grade because I had personal things going on in my life, and I was going through puberty. The interesting thing about my menstrual cycle is that it showed up two years before I came into puberty. I started it my last day of eighth grade for one day, and it never appeared again until I was fifteen and a half years old (strange, to say the least, but I was happy). I wasn't like most girls where they had physical and emotional problems from it. I was a pleasant, very happy, laughing/smiling all the time and the most thoughtful person when I was menstruating.

Sidenote: it changed my personality like a happy drunk when nothing gets to them, and they say what they want and don't care (laughing). Well, I always said what I felt, so maybe that part didn't change (grinning).

To be perfectly honest, I just really wanted to be left alone (a cry that something was wrong), but that never happened. I was in so many extracurricular activities (some by force, others by want). I took piano lessons (three years), gymnastics/acrobatics (four years), tap (six to seven years), jazz (two years), played basketball (only in school), and a member of the Young Adult NAACP Choir (four years) which took up time after school as well. The choir was formed by my ninth grade class under the direction of Trini and support from some parents (the reign was only during high school). This really gave me some pleasure because I loved to sing but as a group, not a soloist (although I did lead a few songs here and there). I felt I had the voice, but my shyness would get the best of me. Oh yeah, rejection was a major distress for me during my teens and some young adulthood!

At the same token, my name states that I am a nonconfrontational and a conflict-free individual, so with a distressful moment, I may have been a walking time bomb (just kidding.) I have a personality where it takes a lot to get me out of character. However, when I did reach my boiling point, oh my, I did not want to talk about it because you were going to make me even more annoyed; so I just wanted to fight. I always felt that talk was cheap, and if you can dish it out, then you better be able to back it up, period! I do remember walking away from many situations where I thought it might get out of control because ultimately, I'd get so agitated I would black out. I did not like for that to happen because I really couldn't afford to get in trouble with the future that I wanted to pursue. So I found ways to stay objective!

Most of the drama I had was over envy anyway (young-minded girls causing unnecessary drama). Sometimes—really all the time—young-minded boys would boost themselves up with these girls about me (confused), and I would be implicated in some mess that very rarely had anything to do with my own actions (boys cause drama too). At times, I wouldn't even know what was going on and walk right into an ambush (more frequent than enough). It was preposterous! I just always remembered what I was told from my family about arguing and fighting. They stressed to me my entire upbringing, never to let them see fear/sweat, and if it comes to fighting, always fight the biggest one first, and all you need is one good punch. I live by this motto too!

Fortunately I was petrified to fight girls because I always thought I would hurt them bad or possibly kill them because I was so heavy-handed and had a powerful punch (just mean-spirited and built-up frustration.) However, I would fight a boy with no questions asked. I had to fight with many of my nephews and their psychotic friends (not literally, I just called them that because they got on my last nerve). Oh, my bad, adults say kids don't have nerves to get on (laughing!). By fighting and tussling with them, I became stronger, wiser, quick on my feet, and could outsmart you at any given moment. This is a good characteristic to be able to convey up! You can't imagine the strength I had mentally and physically for a young girl who only weighed about 80–100 lbs. throughout junior high and high school. Fortunately I was never really in any fights because I would mostly walk away, unless you hit me first which not too many folks would try. They would talk but never any real action. Talk, in my eyes, was just a cheap cry out for "I don't really want anything to come off this misunderstanding, but I must act tough" (bizarre, really). The few fights I was in happened because of someone bothering a family member/friend, and I was taking up for them (kinfolk leaving the scene when I arrive). All I could do was shake my head at their nonsense on both parts. I had an uncontrollable temper when you took me there (oh, and how they really tried to take me there), blacking out sometimes because I was so livid. This did not happen often because I ultimately had a reputation to uphold!

I do remember, when I started driving, my mom telling me that I was not allowed to put anyone besides family in the car and not to get into any accidents because insurance was too high for me at that age. So she would let me drive her car which was a gold manual gearshift Volkswagen Golf, but she had to know everywhere I was going (ridiculous at the time but very appreciative today). I would tell folks I couldn't ride them around, and they would get mad, but I wasn't facing my mom if something would have happened to her car while on my watch (smiling). I would argue with some of them then realize that the car was mine, and I'll ride whom I like! I was not having to face my mom if something happened while the car was in my possession. I was very obedient when it came to my mom (respectful). I believe they respected me later in life for it!

I can also remember having drug dealers as associates for protection because I never knew who wanted to harm me, so I kept them close so they would watch out for me. Oh no, I never dated a drug dealer (that I know of). You best believe that I was not dumb but very clever. I made sure they were never on the job while I was around, and if they did, I had already warned them that I was not taking the fall for anyone, so I would be a snitch. It never came down to that because I think they respected my honesty and respected my family. When they even asked for a ride, I would make them empty their pockets before getting into my car. I was so serious with mine!

Confrontation and I did not get along! My mom was not going to kill me for me not obeying her and having folks in her car. I was not going to let that happen, and they never compromised our relationship by putting me in any harmful situation. Remember, I really kept to myself which is a leadership characteristic! I had hopes and dreams, and nonsense—not of my own will—was going to change my outcome. I keep an individualized aspiration for my success in my mental Rolodex!

INDIVIDUALIZED ASPIRATIONS

Those who try to do something and fail...are infinitely better than those who try to do nothing and succeed.

—Unknown Author

After graduating, I wanted to go to Clark University in Atlanta, Georgia, or A & T University in Greensboro, North Carolina, but my mom was scared for me to go because I was shy and didn't like making friends. She told me I could go if we knew someone in those areas. She did have a friend there, but he passed away when I was at the end of my eleventh grade year. I was so disappointed because I did not want to stay close to home to go to college. I wanted to experience the college life, but I wouldn't have liked it, my mom said, because I was too independent and did not like to share my space with others. I just knew these two colleges had engineering, and that's what I wanted to study. However, I went to Penn State University, Fayette County, instead. I did have my scholarship to the main campus, but there were mostly Caucasians, and I wanted to get away from that environment because I really did not trust many of them. My theory was if I must be around all whites, I might as well stay closer to home. I wasn't trying to offend anyone, but I wanted to experience diversity! At state college, the only diversity I was getting in 1992 was from the football and basketball teams, and that was still few to none. I was itching to see how other diversity campuses were structured or how it felt to be around someone who looked like me. Nope, that never happened; Penn State Fayette campus was where it was going to stay! I did regret not going away to college, though, because I had nothing to converse about when I would talk to other graduates.

While attending Penn State, I really did not do my very best for a couple of reasons: it felt like an extension from high school; too much drama came with going to school close to home; and because I didn't want to be there, I did not give it my all when I received my AS in business administration specializing in marketing (1995). However, when I went back for my BA in letters, arts, and sciences with a concentration in liberal arts in 1996, I was determined to graduate with at least a 3.5 GPA. Oh, how I wish! I did not make that goal mark because some of my associate coursework were added, but I did graduate with a B average. However, I knew then that I wanted and needed to pursue my master's degree once I left Uniontown and worked for a year in a specific career choice.

I was undecided on the career path I wanted to take. At first, I wanted to be a cosmetologist, but my mom said I would not want to stand on my feet all the time, and I couldn't tell people I didn't feel like doing their hair because I was tired (giggling). She knew me because I was very moody like that! Yeah, I would not have liked standing on my feet for hours on someone's head every day either. My mom encouraged me to get a business degree, and after that, I could seek what I wanted, but a business degree can be used anywhere. I guess she really didn't think I was going to stick with being an electrical engineer either. She never even mentioned it! I was very indecisive when it came to my career. I did change my degree three times before deciding on business (engineering, general studies, and undecided). I just knew I wanted to go to college and just go to work. I had forever to work, but I needed the education to get a better job and career in something I really wanted to do. I eventually figured out that the only way I was going to be successful was to own my own business so that I could utilize all my skills and make a breakthrough in some realm of society.

During the summers, I worked for the Private Industry Council from sixteen years old until I was twenty-one years old (I loved it). My very first job was working as an assistant secretary for Judge Franks at the Fayette County Courthouse (did a good job but wasn't what I could pursue as a career). Then every summer after that, I worked as a field monitor which I loved. I did not have to sit in the office, and I was out checking on summer workers working at different sites throughout Fayette County. I knew then that I had to be independent and flexible in the career I chose at that point. I did not want to be micromanaged because it would not be a good fit for me to have to work in that environment. I needed a career where I could manage my own time, at my own pace without someone looking over my shoulders. Just tell me what you want me to do, and I will get it done quickly. I knew young that I could work for four hours and get all my work done for the day. I was not an eight-hour-a-day employee, but I knew that's what I'd have to do, so I better get prepared or get into a leadership position. Needless to say, I may work longer hours to produce productivity, but I am making money that will go in my pocket. It's all mine!

While in college, I worked as a greeter in a sporting goods store in Uniontown Mall, but I was only hired because I was a beautiful young black girl (couldn't believe it), at the game store in the mall as a greeter and salesperson (again hired because of my looks), East End United Community Center as an instructor/tutor for grades K-6, and cities and schools as an at-home tutor for high school students. You can see that I found out early that my looks were going to be a problem because I didn't want my looks to get me employed but my education and experience. This was something else I had to embrace because if I was going to move after graduation, I had to learn how to display my credentials, not my looks (selling my mind and work ethics). However, in this society, beauty gets you in the door, then sometimes you get the opportunity to show off your talents and skills (unfortunate). I am not a person who ever wanted to be looked at as a sex symbol, but I was and that was hurtful. It took me a long time to wrap my head around it (low self-esteem renders its naughty head once again). It still bothers me to a degree, but I am much more and can offer much more than my looks. Respect who you are!

My First Career

In November 1997, I began attending the New United Baptist Church in Southeast, Washington, DC, where Rev. Darin Freeman was pastor. He was looking to open a childcare center in the church and needed an assistant director (director, really). During one of our new member's orientation session, he asked me what I wanted to do because my big-mouthed sister Marilyn told him I was looking for a job, but I really didn't know at the time what I wanted to do, but I was tired of sitting at home with nothing to do. Job hunting in the nation's capital is hard!

I knew I did not want to go into the field of education, but he asked me to give it a chance. He agreed to help me because he really didn't know what to do either. He had known enough people that he could inquire if I would help him. I just kept thinking that I did not have any idea what to do with babies (two to five years old), but since I needed the job, I was up for a temporary challenge. It took me a few days to think about it, but then I told him that I would give him five years, then I had to move on. So we shook hands on it!

Pastor Freeman had many dreams for his church, and a child-care center was one of them. He was a Libra like me but short, bald, arrogant, and very self-assured. I always looked at him like he was just another man (my big brother, really) rather than the pastor. Which made it easy for us to get along so well. We had so many traits, temperaments, and tendencies that it was sometimes scary; we thought so much alike.

I was not interested in being in education because I grew up surrounded by educators on my father's side, and I did not want that stigma. I had no interest in working with children or being an educator, period! But it was a foot in the door, and I appreciated the opportunity, so I gave it a chance. Pastor Freeman must have seen something in me that I did not. He would always say if I were a male, I would be him and vice versa. We were more like brother and sister. When he wanted something done, he told me or gave me a suggestion, and I just ran with it. We worked best that way! I can honestly say, I gave it my all!

On January 8, 1998, The New United Baptist Church Child Development Center (later called The New United Christian Academy) opened its doors from the ground up. I put in long diligent hours and was very dedicated because this would ultimately make or break the reputation I needed to build in this new city.

I don't like failing, so I did everything to the best of my ability. It brought out characteristics I never knew I had. Yes, I was the assistant director on paper but six credits short of being the director. So during the summer of 1999, Pastor Freeman talked me into enrolling in the University of the District of Columbia to obtain the courses I needed to be the director since I was doing all the work. I did just that and no more because I did not want a degree in education. I knew I really didn't want anyone else receiving accolades for work that I put in while acting as the director. I did not like compliments, but I would accept recognition for work I had done.

I learned everything I could learn to make the center shine. All other center director's put their nose down at me and did not want to help, but that was okay. I was a college graduate, and I knew how to work a computer. I set it in my mind that I was going to outshine these old timers, and ultimately, I did, to a degree. I figured if you were not willing to help me, I would gladly help myself succeed as I am growing. My mom used to always say, "One monkey doesn't stop no show!" I kept that thought through every obstacle I was faced with in early care and education. It has worked for me!

At the beginning, I did not think I wanted to make a career working with children, but I stayed as the director until we closed in February 2008. During my tenure, we went from three children to our capacity of sixty in less than a year. We received vouchers (subsidy) from the Department of Human Services (DHS) and reimbursement for food from the Child and Adult Care Food Program (CACFP) by USDA. I accomplished becoming the first level 1 bronze center to achieve National Association of Education for Young Children (NAEYC) accreditation in 2002, going from bronze to gold in less than four years. I was successful with the help of dedicated employees and surrounding myself with good people who believed in me. In 2003, we became a level 2 center where we could enroll subsidized families at the center instead of referring them to the DHS office. This also meant that we could keep all parent fees owed instead of the government including it in the reimbursement amount we get per child.

In 2005, I wrote a grant to house one pre-K classroom in our faith-based facility. We received the grant, and we became the first faith-based pre-K pilot through the Department of Human Services (DHS) to house sixteen pre-K children between the ages of three to five years old. This was an initial pilot program which was on a year-to-year basis which meant you had to keep applying or at least maintain quality. We held this classroom for two years before closing (2005–2007). It was hard finding three-to-five-year old children who were not attending public school. Families wanted their children in a public school environment so they wouldn't feel like babies. Other families just wanted to sit at home and not work if they did not have to while their children were at school. See, with this program, you did not have to work for the pilot, but if you wanted before and aftercare, you had to be working or in school. The biggest struggle to fulfill thus far!

When we achieved it, we were amazed at how well respected we became—from just being me and the staff working hard with our families and children. I gained some popularity with government officials in childcare, other directors, and those who just heard about what achievements I did for New United. I'm not big on compliments, but we (staff and me) did a good thing! I am glad I was blessed with a good leadership style!

Since the government regulations and NAEYC qualifications for teaching staff was changing in 2005, I talked all of my staff into attending college to receive their AA degrees in child development, and I would seek my PhD in clinical psychology because I did not like the fact that they were putting all our black boys on medication, and I wanted to stop the trend. I felt they needed more stimulation, not medication. So I went to study the mental state of African American boys through clinical trials of stimulation rather than medication. In addition, I wasn't going to ask my staff to pursue a career, and I didn't enhance my own. We were a *team*!

The staff trusted and respected me so much that they went to school against most of their will, but they knew it would lead to a better future for them. They could grow into better teachers at New United or work in public school, if it came to that. They would have credentials to market themselves in this fast-paced field. I felt like a proud mommy when they all stuck with it and graduated!

In 2007, I became pregnant with my son and outgrew being a director because I did not think I could take it any further, because we fell into financial problems and the interim pastor did not want the childcare center. We opted to close the doors permanently after being open for ten years on February 28, 2008. It was a hard reality to swallow after ten years of us putting in our blood, sweat, and tears, but I knew we did not have the means to challenge the closure. Plus I really was burnt out and did not want the challenge.

In addition, Pastor Freeman, who talked me into it, was gone, and I felt I could honor him by growing in another aspect of childcare or education, period. Maybe I would open my own Montessori school or charter school since they were becoming popular, and I would have a PhD to run it successfully. The field of education was changing and not all in a positive manner. I thought I could help more on the outside, and I just did not really know if my heart was in education anymore. I was undecided on my next adventure with my career. Since I had started consulting with other centers, I took a risk at becoming a consultant (education).

My Second Career

However, while still the director, I ventured out to open my own consulting business in 2006; it was called Tracy's Consulting Group where I would work with other centers with training, coaching, mentoring, technical assistance, and achieving national accreditation. This was just a hobby, I thought, but it turned into something I started to love. I see myself running a consulting firm in the future with many different avenues for individuals and groups to get assistance.

As a consultant, I have the opportunity to contract work out, train professionally on topics related to childcare, reject jobs I don't feel are a good fit, travel, network, and learn and grow as I am succeeding. Consulting can be challenging as well because you must make enough money to still live comfortably, if not more. To be the most successful, I had to love what I did and put my best foot forward at all cost because this was how my family would survive. At first, it seemed a little backward for me because I did not want to just stay in education, but it opened doors I would have never had the opportunity to see if I hadn't been open to new challenges and situations.

The closing of one door opened a new chapter in my life that I was ready to see how I was going to conquer it. I always enjoy pushing myself to the limit when it comes to learning and work experience. I get an adrenaline rush when I run into a challenge, it's refreshing! Unfortunately when I think I have run my race, it's time to move on. That's just my personality! I'm still running my own business! We will talk more about what I am doing today in the next book (smile). Keep a lookout! I have a third, fourth, even maybe a fifth career now (wink wink).

MATURITY

When life puts you in tough situations, don't say "Why me?"
Just say "Try Me!"

—Unknown

I was always told I was very mature for my age, no matter what my age was at the time. I just always thought because my parents were older, and I had older siblings, that was the reason I acted a little more mature than my peers. However, I don't really know when my maturity level became a discussion. I can remember always having a strong head on my shoulders, but I just thought it was normal. I can say that I was mature in school but not common sense. Maturity comes with experiences and exploration. I wasn't a follower, so I didn't get into trouble, but as I was getting ready for college, that's when my maturity question arose.

College life was when I really found out my maturity level. Maybe it was after I graduated from high school period, but in between high school graduation and my first semester of college, I was tested. It started with me trying to select a college and wanting to work while in college. I witnessed many individuals accomplishing both, but I never knew how difficult it could be because I still had to keep up with my course assignments. When I chose to do both, I was basically setting myself up to either sink or swim! Professors do not care about your personal life—they want their work completed and on time no matter what the circumstances. I did not have to learn that the hard way! Remember, I was a nerd, so I had no choice but to study and do my work, or I would fail. Unfortunately learning did not come easy to me, but I worked at it so that now I can manage it successfully without anyone noticing.

As you read, I chose to attend college close to home, but it was only because I could not attend the colleges I really wanted to. My mom and family were questioning my maturity level, but young people go away to school all the time, so what was the big deal with me? I guess it was because I had more book smarts, but I was lacking in the common sense area. My family just believed I was too naive to move to a big city after high school, but I wasn't a follower, so I did not understand. I knew my boundaries and limits way too well at eighteen years old to have people trying to convince me into an act that I would ultimately get a negative result. I believe my mom felt I wasn't ready. I felt with all the guidance from my parents, my siblings, and all the other influential adults in my life that they had planted the seeds, so now it was time to see me blossom. I regret that I'll never know how college life really is, though (a little sad). My mom has a grip on me! Sometimes I think a lot of it is double standards, but what am I to do but grow and prove I am mature enough to hold my own experiences and challenges.

The definition of maturity is the quality or state of being mature (having or showing the mental and emotional qualities of an adult; having a fully grown or developed body: grown to full size; having reached a final or desired state); full development; perfect condition (http://www.merriam-webster.com/dictionary/mature). In many cultures, maturity is determined by parents and society which have a different perspective as to the individual themselves. Maturity is a significant part of your overall character as well as when you become an adult. This is something that you learn through your many experiences in life.

Maturity can be determined by how you handle situations that challenge your actions on a specific level. It is also a test if you have what it takes to be taught in this busy world and survive successfully even through hard times. Unfortunately it takes discipline to want to keep learning and adjusting to life's changes in each career you choose, or just life in general, which creates your maturity level. Although you have become an adult, it does not mean you have reached your maturity level or are mature.

After reading the definition of maturity, I can see why there was some skepticism in me moving to a large city right out of high school. I can also understand that they were just trying to protect me and mold me a little bit more so that I would be ready for life's many obstacles. If I had moved too fast, things may have gone left for me instead of right, and I can live without knowing what could have happened (smiling).

So for me, to express my maturity, I decided to move to Washington, DC, in search of my career success and independence. I also really needed to know who I would become so that I could someday give back to society. Boy, oh boy, was this a major decision and transition for me! It was not going to be easy at all because I chose to move with my needy sister—that's what we call her. I was used to living under my parents' rules, which was cool because it really did not bother me. Plus as I got older, rules weren't really rules anymore, it was respect.

Holy smokes, here I go living with my sister and her new husband who did not have any children in the house, and she did not work. Oh, what a night (as they say)! Now I was twenty-two, about to be twenty-three years old, and my sister and her husband come up with rules as they deemed fit (strange). It was a major adjustment! It was already strange moving from a rural town to a big city where people were out for themselves. But having rules to follow at your leisure because it's your house was a bit much for me. These actions made me realize I had to mature very quickly and move on my own, period!

I moved on August 15, 1997, to Washington, DC, the chocolate city. I decided to relocate to the District of Columbia, Maryland, and Virginia area because there would be many job opportunities; and since my sister did not have any children, I would not be held back with babysitting. Well, that was short-lived because it was hard to find a job outside of the government if you had a degree and work experience, and my sister was up all night.

I knew I didn't want to go into the government because I didn't think I could grow in a career of my satisfaction. I did not like to be micromanaged. I was used to working where the supervisor gave me my duties, and I went to work. I did always finish early, but I liked to go to work and get the job done, not to socialize. My sister, being up all times of night, was a major distraction because I liked to be alone. She would sleep all day and be up all night on the computer. She would holler for me to come see what she was doing in the early hours of the morning. I was miserable to say the least! I love my sister, but this was just too much! I basically cooked, cleaned, and watched TV most of the time because I was bored. I needed a job quick, fast, and in a hurry because I was getting in the habit of sleeping which would be hard making the adjustment once I started working.

With the help of others, I applied for jobs, but I was either over-qualified or not qualified enough. This helped me accept being told no, which is a good quality for a mature person to possess. I applied for all types of jobs, even though I knew I might not want to be in that career. I just needed to get my foot in the door then I'd go from there (a mature young lady). I was not going back to Pennsylvania, so I was going to make something happen! If I would have had to go back to Pennsylvania, that would have been catastrophic for me during this time. I needed a game plan that could make it easy for me to get a job. However, it was far from easy. The individuals in the DMV area have many crabs-in-a-barrel mentality. Fortunately for me, I loved a good challenge because it just makes me stronger. I will push, press, and progress to the highest power when I am faced with rejection. I am not a quitter!

So I applied at FedEx but was denied the position because I had a college degree and individuals with degrees don't stay at man-ual-labor jobs for long. Well, that's what I was told by a supervisor there, and I scored too high on the test. I was so distraught because I thought they just wanted employees they could manipulate because they could not make that kind of money anywhere else without a degree (slavery). I also felt this was discrimination, but what was I to do because I really didn't want to be a delivery person or do customer service work (now I'm being picky without a job at all [giggling]). So I applied at UPS, private sectors as a secretary (I really don't have phone etiquette, but I can file [laughing]), and as a sales representa-tive (a skill I'm not sure I possess), but I needed a job. I would have taken anything after four months of having no luck.

I just kept thinking, I had to grow up very fast if I was going to stay in the DMV area and succeed. I found out quickly that the DMV area was not for newcomers with an education, not in the political realm, or not really knowing anybody. To get ahead in this city, you must have someone vouch on your behalf, and that might not even work. It was a terrible feeling and example of life for me because I assumed, we (black people) would stick together. Oh, how I was so, so wrong! Blacks are their own worst enemies in cities because they have trust issues, and since they had to work for what they have, they want future generations to do the same. Some do set up situations to help us, but most do *not*! We are the only cultural group that acts this way (sad). I made it up in my mind that I was going to change that thought process. I believe a mature individual helps their fellow man get ahead if they have the opportunity and means to do so. Maybe that was my upbringing, though, but I felt mature individuals don't worry about what others have; they try to help their brothers and sisters because they already knew the struggle. I had a lot of growing up to do when I chose to move to Washington, DC.

I kept thinking that I did not want to work where my looks played a part because that would have been a serious problem after a while (flashbacks to Pennsylvania). I also kept thinking growing up isn't as easy as some people make it look because you are on your own, pretty much. This was when I noticed I was still naive when it came to certain things because I was receiving a serious reality check. A young woman from a little rural town in Southwestern Pennsylvania, where everyone was friendly and knew each other, moving to a place where people did not want to see you more successful than them (Southwestern Pennsylvania has become more like the city now). This was a very hard pill to swallow! I had to put my mature face on and master the challenges I would face with great anticipation that I would be successful. I want to see all my brothers and sisters succeed if I can help it because it only makes us more powerful as a people (a mature thought).

I am still maturing every day, but I know it will get easier. Life throws many obstacles in your path to see if you will conquer or fail, and I am not a quitter, so I will keep pressing on. I am finding out that maturity comes from experiences, not just a physical aspect but both physical and mental. We all can stand to mature more personally and professionally! Remember that just because you become an adult does not mean you are mature. It is your mental state and actions that determine your maturity. You cannot mature if you do not understand your existence to learning which ultimately helps you grow!

THE EXISTENCE OF LEARNING

Climb mountains not so the world can see you, but so you can see the world.

—Unknown

Why do we need to learn? Why are some more eager to learn than others? How do we get the best understanding of the concept for learning? Is learning as important as most people say it is? Is it a stigma we place on people?

I bet if you asked these questions to ten individuals, you will get ten different answers. This is the uniqueness about the existence of learning. My definition of learning is what I make of it and how I use it to better my conceptual thoughts and feelings. For me, learning is so much more than the books, environment, experiences, and social media. I love to learn and understand the thinking process of individuals. My theory of learning is so dynamic in a sense that one usually cannot conceptualize what is beyond their memories or thoughts. The best theory for learning is believing in owning your own thoughts and generating them into pieces of material which can be utilized to better communicate with individuals of like and unlike minds.

My ancestors had to die over wanting their rights to a good education and learning. Most of them were lucky, but many gave their life for the future of learning across generations. We take learning for granted, but it's not what knowledge you possess but how you use it for the betterment of yourself and mankind. I never really liked to read but loved to learn. However, as I mature, I have learned that reading is more important in understanding what you learn and how you learn to retain the most valid parts of your learning style. Fortunately learning is not just a job for me, it is the productivity I receive from its power I gain! For me, learning is power that

89

no one can take from me unless I allow them to. Therefore, as you will read, my degrees are different, but they all lead to one common denominator—*me*.

I attended Penn State University of Fayette County, Pennsylvania, to seek an engineering degree but went undecided because Fayette campus did not offer engineering. However, after the second semester, they told me if I wanted to pursue a degree in electrical engineering, I would have to transfer to the main campus at state college in Pennsylvania where I was really accepted with a scholarship.

Oh no! We tried that college life thing, and it did not last so that was not going to be happening. So I changed my major to business administration because my mom said you can never go wrong with a business degree. I graduated with an associate's of science degree in business administration with a marketing specialization in August 1995.

Since school never came easy to me, I just always worked hard at making sure I always did my best. It wasn't a major adjustment for me, but I had to study because if I didn't, my grades would suffer. I struggled with economics and statistics. I ended up needing a tutor to pass. My sister Maria even tried to help me with Statistics because she was strong in that area, but I just could not get it. A young man in my economics class tried to help me with economics, but I found out we were helping each other. I did end up getting a C in both classes. Oh baby, I was happy with that!

I was going to return in September 1995, to pursue my bachelor's degree, but finding out I had glaucoma right before the semester started, I knew I wasn't prepared. So in January 1996, I enrolled back at Penn State to pursue my bachelor of arts degree. Since I just found out I had glaucoma, I thought I would study something in the medical field concerning the different drugs that could cure eye diseases. However, that would have meant I needed to study pharmaceuticals, pharmacy, or medicine, and those were not courses that were offered at Fayette campus. In addition, I really did not know what the coursework for these areas of study would contain, so I did not want to take the risk. My GPA could not handle any more downfalls! However, learning that I was just a B student was heartbreaking to me because I studied so much and tried so hard. Remember, I said learning did not come easy to me. So I should be grateful because it was hard. I am not!

At this time, Penn State was experimenting with different degrees they would offer and created a letters, arts, and science bachelor's degree in liberal arts. I jumped at it since they did not offer the degree I needed, and I wasn't going to state college. This also gave me the opportunity to explore different courses and areas of study. It gave me flexibility which most degrees didn't offer. So I created my own course load which consisted of classes in different subject areas, and they referred to it as liberal arts on the letters, arts, and sciences course tracks. This bachelor's degree was interesting because I didn't have to stay with a specific course load, and it helped me become more well-rounded personally and professionally.

In May 1997, I graduated with my bachelor of arts degree in letters, arts, and science with a concentration in liberal arts. In my eyes, I could have done better, but with the drama, harassment, and my own mental state, I did my best. I felt with everything I went through, it was the best I could do under the circumstances. I am not a B kind of gal at all, I always shoot for As, but I just couldn't juggle personal issues and attending school living at home where it felt like high school all over again; just the coursework was different. I had so much drama in school and outside of school over the same issue, it was just way too much. A situation I should have not been a part of from the beginning, but girls have young minds and allow boys to taint them all over nothing (shaking my head in disgust). I handled it to the best of my ability, but harassment is no joke when you are trying to better yourself. It would be called bullying today! I kept thinking, *This was the biggest mistake of my life, attending a college close to home.* Oh, how I regret a lot of it, but I did graduate, so that was a positive, and it gave me a chance to get out of some of my naive ways.

When I moved to the District of Columbia, I attended the University of the District of Columbia in Washington, DC, to obtain credits in child development in the summer of 1999. I did not pursue an official degree in it because I was not interested in staying in education. In addition, they did not have a master's degree program. I thought it was crazy to have two bachelor's degrees, but I see a lot of individuals who get them today. It's still a waste of money in my eyes!

I waited a few years, then I enrolled in Trinity College, now known as Trinity University of DC, to pursue a master's degree in education administration and science in 2001. I obtained this degree by going to school one weekend out of the month (Friday night, Saturday all day, and Sunday afternoon). It was a cohort program for working educators who wanted to seek a master's degree in education. This degree can be used to become a curriculum specialist, principal, director of a charter school, or master teacher in supervision. Now I believe you can do more with it, but I never looked back once I graduated on May 18, 2003. Yes, I graduated in two years with my master's degree, only taking classes one weekend out of the month. I initially pursued it so that I could become a principal. I had the business degree, arts degree, and now a master of business and arts degree. I had what it took to sell myself in even more areas of study if I chose.

As you can see, my existence to learning is an ongoing process for me that only I can understand. There is something about knowledge or gaining knowledge that keeps me so intrigued in learning. I can't really explain it, but my actions show that I love to learn and build on my knowledge consistently.

Therefore, when I went back to work in September 2005, from my maternity leave, the field of education was changing again. Now they wanted all teachers to obtain their AA degree to work in childcare because they now were concentrating on the field being known as early care and education. If they were going to change the name and face of childcare, they had to change the perception to higher quality of learners. Wow, I thought to myself! You are trying to change the perception but without the finances. This is going to be interesting! I figured it would flop in about five years, and they would have to revamp it to fit the quality of staff they preferred.

The government also put mandates on centers that they had to go through something referred to as national accreditation (NAEYC, NECPA, NAELL, and NAFCC) to feature high-quality care for children birthed through five years old at their childcare centers or childcare homes. So I knew for me to maintain compliance with the government, I needed my staff to seek an associate degree. Me being who I am, I made a deal with my employees that if they went to further their education, seeking an associate's in child development, that I would enroll in a doctorate program to seek a PhD. Now at the time, I was indecisive in what I wanted a PhD in, but I would go if they went. We could be in school together, and no one would feel slighted.

Since I was having issues with doctors prescribing or diagnosing black boys at an early age with attention deficient hyperactivity disorder (ADHD), I wanted to pursue a PhD licensure clinical psychology degree so I could own my own clinical practice. I was very concerned with the future of our black males, so I wanted to do something about it. Yes, I understood that my degree would take five years compared to my employees' three years, but we were in it together. It was going to be a challenge for all of us, but I knew we could do it because we passed every obstacle they placed in front of us for years, and this would benefit all of us.

In June 2005, I enrolled in Walden University which is a distance learning or online-degree program. I knew I was not going to be able to sit in a class and listen to a professor lecture and students asking questions, so distance learning best fit my learning style. I worked better those days at my own pace as well as on my own. Traditional learning just was not for me at this stage in my life. I probably was always like this, but it was never offered until now, and I jumped on it. The ladies enrolled in Southeastern University together in September 2005. I was so proud of us for wanting to better ourselves. We were a young group of educators, and we had a lot to offer in the education field.

They went kicking, screaming, and complaining, but they all graduated in May 2008, with an associate's of arts degree in child development. I, on the other hand, had two more years to go, but I wasn't going to stop. If they could finish so could I! Unfortunately I became ill and could not finish on time, but I would get my PhD in psychology. It may not be in clinical, but industrial/organizational psychology with a concentration in forensic was looking pretty favorable in 2016. I would be enrolling back in Walden to complete what I started. I would not leave this undone because I have come too far. Knowledge is just enlightening!

Over the years, I have received certificates or recognition in child development associate (CDA) for preschool, IQ testing, certified professional food manager proctoring, American Red Cross first aid/CPR/AED, substitute teaching, early care and education developmental screenings, environmental screening, CDA instructor, professional education trainer, motivational speaker, coaching/mentoring, class observer, and adjunct professor. I look forward to many more opportunities to enhance my existence of learning for not only myself but my children and individuals I encounter. Education should be mandatory at all levels and ages! The more you learn, the more you know it is a great reality check point!

Sidenote: a career in early care and education is starting to become stagnant for me because I feel I have done all I can now. I think I am moving in the direction of motivating, mentoring, coaching, and psychology. I want to work with preteens to young adults because I think that's where change occurs without notice.

REALITY CHECK

In youth we learn; in age we understand.

—Marie Von Ebner-Eshenbach

Many of us don't really want to come face-to-face with one's own reality. Sometimes because it's a hard pill to swallow, it could be devastating, it could alter your character, or it could show you someone you don't want to be or did not want to become. My reality check takes on many different facets because they were looked at as experiences, not a reality (somewhat). A reality check is not something you can take back, but it is something you can change or enhance. No one is exempt from a reality check!

I think my first reality check happened in high school. I wanted to run for prom queen since I was in eighth or ninth grade, and only my closes friends knew that. I did not share it with too many people because of jealousy or cruel acts, so I shared it with the people I thought I could trust and would back me up. Now I never wanted recognition for anything, but I wanted to be prom queen or at least try. I don't even know why I really wanted it, but I know I wanted it. So my senior year came, and it was time to start selecting individuals to be prom queen and king. Well, I was attending a predominately white school, but we had more blacks than the other high school. So I knew I had a chance to win since I was the only black who wanted to run. So I thought!

As I said previously, they would always confuse me and Bridgett for some odd reason all throughout our school years. Little did I know she wanted to run for prom queen too, or maybe someone talked her into it since she was a cheerleader, I don't really know. Well, I found out that Trini nominated Bridgett, and a few others nominated me because they knew that's all I ever wanted to be a part of in high school. I felt like this was a stab in the back! Why would they select the both of us to run when there were not enough blacks to even make a fair vote? I was so hurt and disappointed! This was when I really stopped trusting anyone—I mean anyone. There is no loyalty among people, I thought, no matter how long you know them or what you do for them! Loyalty is gone! So when the day came for us to vote, I voted for Bridgett, and she became second runner-up. I did not want to compete with her, and we were the only two blacks selected. To me, that was pointless! If she wanted it, she could have it because I was not going to challenge her over it. It was just prom queen! However, I did change my thinking and character after this incident. I did not want to have individuals as close friends, just associates, and I did not put my trust in anyone. I believe I went into my shell and did what I had to do for me. No more being responsible for outside of my family's feelings ever again. I was done! I kept my feelings inside a brick wall I created for myself so no one could ever get in. I would never express my feelings toward another person ever again, and I meant that with all my heart and soul.

I remained their friend, but it was never a close friendship. I kept them at arm's length. I did not trust them any longer, and I wasn't going to act like that did not hurt me. I was angry for a long time behind this and just changed my circle of friends altogether after high school. What did I need enemies for when I had friends smiling in my face and stabbing me in the back at the same time? What a reality check, huh?

My next reality check happened during my second year in college. I was taken to the emergency room because the left side of my body went numb while I was sitting in the computer lab at school, working on my final paper. Let me thank Aaron for being there because it could have been worse. I was taken to the hospital, but they couldn't seem to find anything and just diagnosed it as stress. I was confused because I don't get stressed. I just brush things off my shoulders and kept going, no worries (so I thought). By the way, I am not a person who cries either (I haven't cried since I was a baby). This was a reality check and a scary moment all at the same time, but I took it and kept going on with my life. I went right back to my classes the next day like nothing ever happened. Really, I didn't like missing school, and I also had finals coming up. My sophomore year was almost over. This happened in spring of 1994.

Becoming face-to-face with glaucoma was a reality check as well but on a very different scale. I could control my eye pressures and chances of me becoming blind by just following the doctor's orders and taking my medicine. This was more of a reality check; lifestyle change for me!

In April 1997, while going through finals at Penn State, I was violated by a person I was very familiar with. Studies have shown that most woman are violated by someone they know, and it is very true; I can attest to that statement. I was flabbergasted that this had happened to me. No, not LaShawn—she could never let this happen to her (disappointed)! I was always cautious of people, but I let my guard down because I thought I knew this person well and trusted him. I never blamed myself for the incident because I knew I did not show any signs that I was the least interested in any type of relationship with him besides going to the same college and carpooling. It was very hard trying to finish my coursework when I still had class with this person, and he was my lab partner. I tried avoidance, but you can't avoid something or someone that is staring you right in your face. I just kept thinking, *I am stronger than this, I can fight this and still live a productive life without anyone knowing what happened* (silent fighter). So that's what I did! I can never step a foot in his house again, never!

I never told anyone and have gone through life just as if nothing has happened so I would not trigger a situation I could not control. I do not like confusion or confrontation, so I did not want the drama. So I never forgot, but I gave it to God, and I'm trying to forgive him. Believe it or not, this kind of incident is very hard to forget, even if you forgive, no matter how strong you are in your faith (head nod) or how long ago it happened. It is not something you want to relive over and over again, that's for certain! This could have broken me, and sometimes I think it has in a way.

I knew it was better for God to handle it than for me to put it in my family's hands. Plus I knew my faith in God would give me the strength to get stronger and move on with my life. I believe if I would have gotten family involved, it would have been a *cold case*! I would have never forgiven myself! Yes, it has been a struggle (and still is a struggle) in allowing love and trust into other serious relationships. I believe this will always be an issue for me. That's why after the incident, I did not want to casually date, date at all, or even get serious with anyone again. I felt I was tainted now! My heart was with two people, but I was scared to even let them in. Of all the people who understood me, I knew they would have picked something up, and I couldn't have that, so I pushed them away (scared). The one was away at college, and the other one went to the military. Why my heart was torn, I can't really explain, but these two really did their research to understand me. I never experienced a man wanting to know me and taking their time to understand me since (reality check)!

Another reality check of mine is letting someone go even if it hurts because you don't want to cause them any heartache. When your heart is torn between two people you love dearly, you must let both go. It's not fair to them or yourself if you cover up your feelings. It was already a reality check that I let them break down my wall I built so tight. So if I could not fairly choose, then let them both go and find someone who could love, care, respect, trust, and honor them as they should. They were good to me, I must say that, and helped bring out the best in me. I don't regret letting this reality go because I feel it was best for all involved. This, unquestionably, was a mature thing to do! I was not in the game-playing business and never have been for that matter. Honesty is what I try to live by!

So you know after graduation, I had to get out of town and never look back. I just had to figure out where and when I wanted to escape. Honestly I knew there was nothing for me in Uniontown, Pennsylvania. I knew I had outgrown my little rural town and needed to spread my wings toward my success. Believe it or not, I wanted to move after graduating with my AS in 1995, but I was very undecided as to where I wanted to seek my bachelor's degree. So I stayed until 1997 when I received my bachelor's degree.

After the past three years or so, I was so ready for a change and moving to a big city was the ticket because I was starting fresh. Oh boy, what a reality check this was! City folks' personalities are *nothing* like rural/country folks' pleasantness. They are like vultures, ready to snap at any given moment and never have a good reason. They always have their guards up! A reality check, indeed! At this point I just wanted to get away from ever having to encounter my violator again (ran away). I wanted a fresh start! The main reason was that I needed to grow up, and living at home with my parents, I was not going to grow up. I was spoiled and had no responsibilities. Unfortunately I needed to find out who LaShawn was and what her purpose was here on earth. I thought, *What a wonderful, anxious, pleasant opportunity this was going to be for me*! Somehow reality always wants to show its head in my life (shaking my head).

Yes, I could have worked a regular job in the area or surrounding areas, but I needed out of Pennsylvania period. My mom didn't want to see me leave since I was her baby, but she knew I had to leave if I was going to be someone she could admire. When my dad packed up my little Volkswagen Golf with all my belongings, that was my ultimate reality check thus far because I was leaving the nest to experience the world. Oh, was I in store for some things, I tell you!

Since I was a little girl, we always traveled. So I had a little bit of exposure to city life. We traveled the East Coast from Erie to Florida, Ohio and Michigan areas, many Southern states, but nothing on the West Coast, out of the States, or even the Midwest. There were so many children, and my parents nor their parents had money on hand to take us everywhere. A reality check for me because I always thought we had a little bit of change to live like we had lived, but as you get older, you find out things aren't what they always seem when you are a child with no worries. In addition, my cousin Duke exposed us to historical black college life from ninth grade to twelfth grade. I had exposures, but what I would do with them would be my new reality. I was so ready!

My moving reality check was based on location, children, job opportunity, and if I wanted to live with someone or on my own. My mom did not like the notion of me living on my own at first, so I selected the situation I thought would be the most beneficial for me, and that was with my sister Marilyn and her husband, Calvin, in the DMV area. I was looking for a career I could love as well as grow, learn, and motivate me to be my best self. I didn't just want any kind of career, I was looking for somewhere I could someday manage and call my own. One thing I knew was that I did not want anyone interfering in my career decision because I was the one who had to live with the decision (leadership). Reality is that you want to come into your own ownership because your destiny depends on it!

COMING INTO OWNERSHIP

*You can't expect to be old and wise if
you were never young and crazy.*

—Unknown

I was never interested in dating outside of the black race. Especially since my grandmother and father told me, when I was about ten years old, that I was not permitted to date white boys. It stuck with me! I love my black culture anyway!

As preteens and teenagers, we do things that our peers influence us to do. I was not one of those youngsters. I would preach to you why you should or should not do things and the outcome you could face. I was never a follower! I just watched and let people be who they were just as long as they did not get hurt or hurt anyone else. It was more of me not wanting to embarrass my mom, but mostly because I felt I had a lifetime to do adult things. I always thought if I do adult things when I am a teenager, then what will I look forward to when I become an adult? So I never engaged in adult acts (mostly). I knew that once I turned eighteen, I was considered an adult even though I was technically still a teenager. Anything I did at this point—good or bad—would be judged!

I did start socially drinking when I turned twenty-one years old, but when I noticed that it took a lot of drinking, even hard straight liquor, for me to even get a buzz, I knew then that drinking was not going to be long-lived for me. In my opinion, a woman who gets so drunk and stumbles as she walks is not attractive and is subject to being vulnerable to the ones who may want to harm her. We are ladies, and we need to act like it no matter what! I never smoked or even liked the smell. I always felt I had my reputation to uphold, so most things I found offensive. Now don't misunderstand; I was not perfect, but I did strive to be as good as I possibly could. I did not want that look or be in a position where I was not in control. I had to know what was always happening. I believe when you do too much, situations tend to always get out of your control.

I did have two episodes that I can remember where I had too much to drink and almost fell off the stool because my heel was caught in the chair. I always thought heels and I weren't friends (laughing). I did not like that feeling and decided that would never happen to me again no matter what. However, I started drinking at twenty-one and was done by the time I was twenty-three years old. When I could drink liquor on the rocks without a chaser, there was a problem. In addition, alcoholism runs in my genes, so drinking was not in my destiny. I wanted healthy lungs and liver! So I just stopped cold turkey and because I did not want to continue that path, I wanted to be successful without a tainted past which could hinder my future aspirations. I am a firm believer that your past does not always stay in your past. It will rear its ugly head when you least expect it, so always be honest and true to yourself that it is your past, and you cannot change it; but you can be better than what was in your past.

So when my mom told me I had to move out of Uniontown when I graduated from college because there was nothing there, and I was so much more than what they offered in Fayette County, even though I had a job already waiting for me, I did not think twice about moving. Since my family lived everywhere in the US, I had many places to choose from, but I didn't want to go with anyone who had children. So I selected the chocolate city, thinking I wouldn't have a problem finding a job because everyone looked like me. However, there were successful black people but with a lot of politics (not a strong suit for me) and others not wanting to see you succeed (confusing). I had to own up to it and say I will achieve it somehow.

As you have read, it was hard finding a job when I moved. I applied for all kinds of jobs, even ones I knew would be a challenge for me. Other jobs were just turning me down because I had a degree and work experience. I had to come into ownership that I may have to take the first job that hired me even if I know it's not a career. So that's where working at New United Baptist Church Child

Development Center, later called New United Christian Academy under the direction and vision of Rev. Darin Freemen, pastor and executive director, came into play. He gave me my first opportunity, and I *thank* him for seeing something in me that no one else would even had tried. At one point, I even worked two jobs to prove a point that I could. I did that while going to school and working full-time at the center. It lasted for approximately one and a half years—my point was proven! When you have a degree, that doesn't limit your ability to work hard for what you want, you just learn how to work smart as well.

The childcare center was blessed to keep its doors open for ten years, 1998–2008, with me as their director, going through national accreditation (with great staff support), pilot prekindergarten program through DHS (I wrote a grant for it), District of Columbia Health Services (DHS) level 2, and the Child and Adult Care Food Program (CACFP). We were very successful to be so young in the field, but we kept God first. Rev. Freeman left in 2004, but we kept it going in his honor, mostly for his vision for the Southeast Anacostia community. His vision was always more than just a childcare center, he also wanted a charter school in the community. Even though it was difficult at times, we were there for the children, families, and staff in the community. I took ownership of making sure we strived for the best before ending our reign.

Interesting, I can remember being twenty-three years old, and the older directors did not want to help me, but I prospered anyway and conquered it with God's help (crabs in a barrel) and Rev. Freeman's support. I left them speechless because I wasn't from DC, and I made childcare look different. I really didn't know what childcare really looked like, but I knew I needed to do something that would make us standout and our children rise to higher levels once they moved on.

Eventually some of the crabs started stealing my ideas, but it didn't matter because I can always do better. In addition, I would help anybody who wanted to make their centers better. If I knew something, I had no problem sharing (small-town devotion) since we were all trying to fulfill the same goal of enhancing early care and education. I just took the lead in what I thought was best, regardless of what others may have thought of me. I wanted to succeed, and no one was going to stop me. Since I didn't want to go into education in the first place, I was going to make a positive name for myself in the field (ownership).

My young adult life really consisted of working and trying to gain respect from my elders in the childcare community. I assisted others who were new to the field and also those who needed guidance in maintaining their license. Some people started looking at me suspiciously because I was giving out free advice and assistance. I just was thinking, *We are all reaching for the same goal, so why not help others if I can* (my upbringing)? I wanted everyone to be successful, and there were enough children in the communities, so we did not have to compete for enrollment. The problem existed because families would not maintain their vouchers by working or going to school. This challenge was across the board for centers that depended on subsidy to remain open. The area in which we were located, families did not have the financial means to pay full tuition childcare expenses. The way I constructed my business was shocking for so many. I did not let the government control my outcome, just my progress! God gave me the gift, and I was only being obedient and dedicated!

When considering coming into my own ownership, I am very diligent, focused, and adventurous in my thought process. Understand my ownership is something a good leader possesses, and I have mastered most of it! It is mainly because I plan and stick to it, so I'm not displaying indecisiveness. For my future, I still must face courtship or dating, career enhancement, and life's vital encounters. Courtship was undeniably difficult for me as you will see!

THE ART OF COURTSHIP OR DATING

Happiness does not depend on what you have or who you are, it solely relies on what you think.

—Buddha

My courtship started out rocky and really remained that way throughout my life. Since I had trust issues, I never wanted to be disrespected or really connected to a male because they play too many games and were very disrespectful toward females, even when the female gave her all (that was awful). I know it was due to immaturity, or it was learned, and they did not want to change. Fortunately for me, I essentially stayed in my lane and dealt with my own insecurities.

Courting and dating gave me the chills to even think about it altogether. I didn't want to be heartbroken or experience what heartbreak would be like at all or hurt someone because I could not be obligated to another person. It was like a hold that I could not totally control and did not inevitably want to share my emotions. Honestly I only started because kids would say I was a dyke or afraid of my mom finding out. In the '80s and '90s, it was not acceptable to want to be in a relationship with the same sex. It was shunned upon in the black community! Hell, I just wanted to go to school, get good grades, and grow up knowing how to gain wealth. My mom's opinion wasn't even close to my reasoning not to date. I had my whole life to court and date or maybe just be alone, loving myself! Yes, I did think a lot of boys were handsome and clever but not really neck and neck with me and my future aspirations. They were predominantly older guys too—not too old, though (one to five years)!

I had my first so-called boyfriend at the end of tenth grade. I say so-called because I only started going out with him because peers were getting on my nerves about not having a boyfriend, as I said. You may call this a little peer pressure. I just called it leave me the hell alone! I was only attracted to black guys of the lighter complexion. They weren't necessarily the best looking, but they were at least a 7–8-ish (giggling). Well, in the late '80s and early '90s, lighter-complexioned individuals were in. I don't really know why because there were other boys more attractive than light bright folks. Nonetheless, I was more attracted to caramel, to the color of butter (smiling). They had ego issues once I started really paying attention to them and their actions (ugliness). So this relationship only lasted a year or so because he thought he was a player, and as I said before, I didn't have time for games.

I knew most significant or life-changing situations happened in high school, but I wasn't into being a statistic. I just wanted to be LaShawn and gain much respect from people without negative thoughts of my character. I made it my business to not tarnish my name, and I did not allow others to do it either. Don't lie on me to make you look good because I would certainly call you out on it! I was not scared to take up for myself, that was for sure. I learned that early, very early in school with boys or girls. I let them do it in elementary school a little, but by the time I was in middle school, *no way*.

When I was in twelfth grade, I met Eddie while working at a sporting goods store in the mall. At the time, I was not interested because he was mahogany which was a little dark for me, but he had the most beautiful eyes and whitest teeth I had ever seen on a dark-complexioned person. He was attractive! He was very charming and sweet to say the least, and he had a beautiful smile. He was persistent too. Which I think, with me, you had to be, or you would have been overlooked. I agreed to go to the movies with him, but he had to come to my house to meet my parents first. I will never forget my family's reaction when he came to pick me up. They asked him several times if he was sure he came for me because they had never seen me interested in anyone of his color. They were stunned! We tried to date, but we were better friends. He did like me more than I liked him, but I just thought we would be better as close friends and nothing more.

I was tough when it came to boys and having a boyfriend. When I watched my nephews and brothers, I already knew I had to be cautious. I just always thought they wanted sex, and that wasn't on my repertoire. I was only looking to be friends and no more. They would always want more, and I discovered that after I heard there was a bet going around school that the first boy who can get me to have sex with them would win a notch on their bet because I wasn't interested in having sex, and mainly because I did not want children, and boys were nasty. Remember, I grew up with my nasty nephews always wanting to do adult things with girls. I needed to graduate with an academic diploma, not give out certificates to boys for their immature egos. Unfortunately I lost my virginity at sixteen years old and regretted every minute of it. I did not like it, nor did I get the big deal that everyone was making about it. It was sloppy! I was so disappointed I allowed my curiosity to get the best of me. I should have stuck to not wanting to know! A regret I am going to have to live with.

I lost my preference for skin color once I noticed that all shades of brown are beautiful and sexy. Then I just looked for qualities where we related. Not too many boys rattled my fancy with their intellect, though! I was book smart, little to no common sense, but very observant. So where I may have lacked, I picked it up in another department. A boy could not just think he could talk sweet and get me to crumble because it wasn't happening with me. I gave you the blues if you really were interested in a so-called relationship. It followed me forever! Boys use to say, "Damn, girl, who hurt you that you are so tight!" That wasn't the case! I just knew what I wanted, and they weren't it. It was either I liked you or I didn't, there was not an in between, just like my character (laughing).

I never wanted an interracial relationship of any sort. I just liked black guys! I was prejudiced! It is nothing to be proud of either, but I knew I had a problem because I would get very touched when I saw interracial couples, especially black ladies with white men. My skin would just crawl every time, and my sister had a baby to one, and another sister married one. It was extremely hard for me to ever get over it! It wasn't as difficult to see a black man with a white woman since a couple of my brothers either married or dated them. It just was not for me!

I had these feelings mainly after I started learning about slavery and the black culture regarding whites, and it sickened me that my ancestors were raped and made to have interracial children but still treated them all terrible. Blacks and whites could not drink from the same water fountain nor sit at a counter, but you could have sex and have a baby with us. It's disgusting! I know we should forgive and forget because that was then and this is now, but I can't because those images play in my mind. Plus some of this is still happening today, just in a different form. I did not want to be associated with anyone who was not black when it came to boyfriends. I did not think any other race could understand my struggle. So I would hang out with others, but nothing ever serious (shaking my head). I had a few who were interested in me, but I loved my black guys. Furthermore, I had goals, and boys or being serious with a boy was not prevalent anyway.

However, things changed when I started dating a ninth grader in February 1992, after not really wanting to do it because he was so much younger than me (grade wise but only two years in age). I was about to graduate and go to college, away from Pennsylvania, I hoped, and I did not know what would happen to us trying to get into a serious relationship. But he was very persistent, kind, loving, patient, and easy to talk to about everything. He ended up breaking my wall down and became my first true love (not puppy love). We had a connection I really could not explain.

My family would make fun of us because of his age, but it didn't bother me after a while. I was just very skeptical of wanting more with him because I was older, and I wanted to leave Uniontown forever. He made me feel like I was the most important person in his life, and I felt the same about him. He gave me the nickname, Joule, because he said I was precious like a jewel (sweet). We were very protective of each other and inseparable. We dated steadily for about a one and a half years, then off and on. We always said we were friends first no matter what! This relationship was different for me in so many ways because it was so easy and drama free. We were so comfortable with each other. We even rumored we might get married once we got older because it was so easy, and we got along so well. It was the age that held me back because I did not want him blaming me for him not experiencing life the way he wanted by following me. It was mostly my fault with our relationship because I thought I was preserving a future relationship by allowing us to experience life before we got serious. As the old folks would say, "To sow our rural oats." I loved him unconditionally too, but life takes turns we can't always control sometimes.

We made sure we stayed friends! I was getting ready to graduate from undergrad, and he enlisted into the military which I really did not want him to, but it was his decision because I was making mine. I felt if we were meant to be once we matured, then God would bring us back together. Funny thing, we lost contact for about thirteen years over something petty. That was very hard on me, but I chose to move, and he moved on with his life once he returned from the marines, and I wasn't there. It's a very strange situation, really! I never stopped loving him, and no one could ever take his place in my heart. It is so interesting what the heart does when it thinks you are in love.

There was only one other guy who came close to Michael, but I did not want a long-distance relationship. However, when we were together, he treated me like a queen. I loved it! He never really knew how I truly felt, but I did fall in love with him. I needed someone I could be with when I wanted to and not just during school breaks. We had a good time when we were together, though. The distance between us being at two different colleges did not help us build anything. We just picked up when we could, but I lost contact with him for over twenty years. I kept him as a good friend as well, never really telling him how I felt.

How do you keep male friends as friends if you had feelings for them at some point, is it hard? I reply, I'd rather have their friendship than nothing at all! As I said, sometimes we must let situations go over certain circumstances, but if they are worth it, keep them as friends. For me, most of my male friends have liked me for one reason or the other, but I only dated a couple. Everyone is not worth a courtship! My mom always said, "Watch who you lay with and date because they may not be who you want to spend the rest of your life with." A statement I lived by!

I tried other relationships, but I would always find a reason why I could not make a serious relationship out of it. This was when I noticed I was very selective in wanting guys in my life. I always gave them a hard time, no matter what, because if you wanted me, you must work for it if you think I'm worth the wait. I knew from the males in my family and my sisters that guys only really wanted one thing, and if you just hand it to them, they will walk all over you and not care. I had dreams, so I didn't even want the headache of being responsible for other actions. I was selfish, you can say!

I even had those who said things about me that were not true, but you believe what you want, and I really did not have time for he-said-she-said gossip. Which I found out that guys gossip way more than gals and about things that they should not share; but they think they are hurting me, but I just always thought it made them look more immature. I was a smart butt, so when you tried those jealousy tactics, I ignored you to the fullest. However, I would confront you if I thought it would tarnish my name. I did have my fair share of gossipers, but I never let it get to me unless you would bring harm to me. I can say that I only let three guys in my life who really meant something to me before moving to Washington, DC, where I met a guy who would become my husband (something I was reluctant to do because I wanted to achieve my goals I set for myself as a teenager, and marriage was not in my plans). When you live in a small town, people assume all the girls are "fast," but most are not. The ones who do have those actions are sneaky or really don't care.

He was the third guy I met when I moved to Washington, DC. The other two were just guys who I met through someone else to get me out socializing which is not one of my strong characteristics (smiling). We met because of my big-mouthed sister Marilyn, noticing him staring at me when I was walking to the truck from shopping for shoes for my niece who just moved with us. I never even talked when we met because Marilyn did all the talking for me, which she frequently did. He told us his name was Javon, which we later found out it wasn't nor was he four years older than me. When he gave me his number, I was advised not to call him for a couple days and all these crazy rules (weird). I was not interested in meeting anyone, so it made no difference because I wasn't calling anyway. But he called me that night (annoyed now). Now I had to talk to this person because Marilyn had to open her big mouth. I gave him a hard time from the door. He wasn't giving up, though. He was always coming around between his shifts at work. I did not work at the time but was looking for a job, so he would come over all the time. I would question his motives because it just was not normal to me that someone would want to be bothered with someone who wasn't interested at all and did not act like she was interested. He even knew I had feelings for someone else, and it didn't matter because I wasn't pursuing the person to have a relationship. Later he would throw this is my face (sad)!

I remember he became sick in November 1997, where he couldn't work or do anything, so he called me to take care of him. I did just that! I would take him soup and help him in any way I could since he wasn't up to it. He was sick for about two weeks, and I took care of him. Since we were friends and semidating, I thought it was what a good friend would do in a friend's time of need (foolish later). He asked to go home with me for Thanksgiving, but I really did not want him to because I wanted to see if Michael and I could have something. I just had to make sure of what I was doing before I made a big mistake and would later regret it.

To my surprise, Michael was not speaking to me for some odd reason which really broke my heart because I always thought we would be friends, no matter what. When I saw him in the bar, and he looked at me and ignored me, I was devastated. I couldn't get over it! I never asked him what happened or anything because I really did not like rejection, and I don't think my heart could have taken it. Yes, I was there with Kelvin, but we had only known each other for about four months, so it wasn't serious in my eyes yet. However, Michael's actions really played on me to a point where I got a little depressed. Out of all the people I knew, I never thought, for a moment, that we would end up not talking for years and me not knowing what happened. I had to let it go (it took years, but I never fully let it go in my heart of hearts)!

Christmas 1997, after I met Kelvin, he gave me an I-love-you ring which was a one-carat diamond ring. I was very disappointed because how could you love someone you just met five months ago that much. I wanted a TV, not a ring, and especially not an I-love-you diamond ring. I did not know him that well to make that kind of commitment. I was still in love with someone else, even though we hadn't spoken. I was so confused! As time went on, I grew to love him but not the way he thought and not in a manner where I thought to spend the rest of my life with him at that point. He was moving too fast for me!

However, sometime in 1998, we did look for a wedding ring, but the wedding wasn't going to be for a few years because we really didn't know each other, and I really didn't want to get married or have children still. He had put it on layaway but took it off later on that year because we had a disagreement about me not taking his side when it came to my family, but I told him there is no choosing when it comes to family. You can come and go, but my family will always be my family, period.

He stopped speaking to me for months, then he got sick and wanted me to go take care of him again. I kept thinking that this was not going to work, so I should stop it before it goes any further. But I allowed others to convince me into staying with him. I think I was so hurt that I really wasn't caring too much about a love life. Who I wanted had moved on, and I knew there was nothing I could do now, so I thought we would just date and never get married. That was not in his plans!

In 1999, he moved into his own apartment. At first, I was just spending a lot of time there, so I did not have to stay at my sister's house and listen to her rules. But around April that year, I moved in with him because I had to get out of my sister's house, and he had his own place. We lived together for four years. There were good times and bad times, but every time I wanted to leave, I allowed others to change my mind. I knew he wasn't the one for me because he really didn't understand me. I was very difficult to understand, especially when I don't want you to know the real me. It wasn't a lie, I just didn't feel that connected with him, and he would sometimes use things I told him against me which was not cool. I knew if he loved me as much as he portrayed, then he would never try to hit below the belt. When you truly love someone unconditionally, you do not try to harm them is what I believe. When you try to hurt me, you do not love me, in my eyes, because hurt is not love. In addition, if I don't try to hurt you, then why are you doing things to hurt me? I was so perplexed!

Then my mom got in my ear, saying that we had been living together for four to five years, so we needed to get married, but I did not want to get married. I was not convinced he was the one for me! In addition, I could leave whenever I wanted because I had no attachments. Don't get me wrong, I never made him feel like I did not want to be there that I know of. I was just trying to find myself, and I had dreams that no one really could understand. No matter how strong minded you are, continuous conversations about marriage from people you look up to can get you caught up. They mean well, but you are the only one who knows how you feel!

In 2001, he tore his Achilles heel while playing flag football. He had to have surgery and wore a cast from his toes to his thigh. His leg was bent for twelve weeks in this cast. At the same time, my grandfather was ill with cancer, and I knew he did not have long to live, so I wanted to be with him as much as I could because he was my only grandfather still living, and we were very close. I did go home a few times before he passed, but for the most part, I stayed and helped him. He couldn't do anything for himself, not even walk because of his knee being bent. If we would go somewhere, I had to help him get in and out of the truck, and he was over 250 lbs., and I was about 135 lbs. He had crutches, but I cooked for him, brought his plate to him, and helped him take showers because he couldn't get the cast wet. I did all this and was not married to him.

Once he got the cast off, he developed a blood clot in his lung. It was from having the cast on all that time with his leg bent. The cast was supposed to have been cut down each time he went to the doctors, but they were afraid he would try to do too much, so they left it bent. He was a football and sports junkie! He started complaining about his back hurting first, then he said his side was hurting, and he pointed to his lungs. I knew first aid/CPR, and I knew his complications where not normal. So a week before Thanksgiving, he was rushed to Prince Georges Community Hospital because he was complaining his side was hurting, and it was hard for him to breathe. I stayed with him all day and night the first night because he didn't know what was happening, and he was in a lot of pain. The next day, I went home to take a shower, nap, change my clothes, and he called me because the nurses were not treating him right (so he said). I rushed back to the hospital, and he was half-asleep (shaking my head), talking about he doesn't want to be left there alone. I was tired; I still had to go to work! Then his mom came to spend time with him, so I could go home and get some rest. Meanwhile my grandfather was taken to hospice, and I couldn't make it home because I was with him (upset). He had to stay in the hospital for five days so he could be monitored. I was mad that I could not go home. After he got out the hospital, I went home for my grandfather's services. I was sad I did not get to see him one last time. So I figured God wanted me with Kelvin (depressed/confused) since I stayed with him and did not go see my grandfather.

After seeing some of his actions that I did not agree with, I knew if we would get married, this would be a big problem. There were many things I'd seen and felt, but I was hurt, so I allowed my thoughts to be altered (second-guessing myself). I wasn't who I thought I was anymore because I got tired of fighting and gave in. The debating LaShawn would have never given in, but I just was so hurt and depressed I allowed it. We should have dated a little longer!

I did get two beautiful children from the marriage and gained two amazing stepchildren. I could not be more satisfied with my decision because of these four individuals. Children can change many facets of your life, and now that I must go back out on the dating scene, I must make sure the children are taken into consideration, plus my dog, Bailey.

Courtship is really what you make it, but for me, I know it's going to be a task because I am not the most personable person when it comes to meeting new people who may be a long time part of my life. I am more than likely going to go back to my past. If I must go out in today's world and date, most likely, I will be single. Me attempting to trust someone unknown around my children will never happen. Men usually only want to be with the woman, not bothered with their children. Some may act like they like your children and then do harm to them. This is a crazy time we live in, and I don't have time to invest in a man who can't love me and my children. I won't put myself in a predicament that I have to worry about that. I believe at a certain maturity level, you know what's good for you and what's not. This is part of me establishing my quest in leadership. I must be a leader in my own life before I can bring someone else around. Therefore, these courtship traits have helped me establish my leadership quest.

ESTABLISHING MY LEADERSHIP QUEST

Life is like a camera: focus on what is important, capture the good times, and develop from negatives.

—Unknown

I always showed leadership skills from childhood. I was always the child who would try things but only if I knew the consequences. I would never follow other children or family. I had to do things on my own, but I would try not to spoil your fun (smiling). The one time I chose to be a follower, I received a spanking. I allowed my nephews to talk me into gambling with the pennies my mom saved for us to put in our savings account (we all—twelve or so—had savings accounts my mom started us from birth). After this situation, I was never a follower again; if I did something, it was because I wanted to, not from others.

Leadership skills can be taught, but mostly you are born with it, I believe. Everyone is born with leadership qualities. However, I believe your environment and experiences can change the way you view situations which makes it difficult, sometimes, to remain in that leadership position. As the saying goes, "you can't have more chiefs than Indians," meaning you must have followers in order to be a great leader. If we have all leaders, how will we get the work done we are put here to complete? Therefore, followers must have leadership qualities! How do you know you are a follower if you do not have the qualities to look for?

I noticed many of my leadership qualities improving with my age. I took things very seriously and didn't want to disappoint anyone. I took initiative when no one else would try because I really love challenges and to be challenged. Many situations and circumstances I would participate in was because my mom would take me to her meetings (she was involved in every organization known to man and was, most of the time, the only black, but she never backed down and always spoke her piece), and I would watch how she conducted herself and mimicked some but put my own twist to it, just not recreating the wheel that may only need a small fixing (smiling).

I held many leadership roles in church, in high school, and undergraduate college. I was usually put into these positions because I never volunteered, but I would always give it my all whenever I took the role. This helped me tremendously because as I was growing into an adult, it wasn't hard for me to take control of any situation—good or bad—and turn it around to something spectacular. I do not like leaving things undone if I can help it! I am very truthful and honest which many people view as negative, but I just think, why get into a situation that can be prevented, and you do not make a spectacle of yourself or me for that matter. I perceive myself as a matter-of-fact individual!

For me to be a great leader, I must pay close attention to my inner circle. So when it came time for me to branch out and grow up, I really started to look at the small number of people in my inner circle. Are these individuals going to help me become the leader I am destined to be, or are they here to bring me nonsense? Many friends/associates I have met along the way were here for a season, and some are still around today. I did not befriend many people because I felt I was different, and most people could not relate to me. I never give up no matter what because leaders never quit until their work is done.

When I started working with Pastor Freeman, he showed me more leadership skills and how to deal with criticism in the workplace and adversity, which I would encounter sooner than I thought because I was young. This was when I knew I had the characteristics to be a great leader. I was taken by the hand by Ms. Keys, she was a light-skinned lady with big red glasses, and almost everyone in childcare feared her but me. While Ms. Powers (God rest her soul), a woman who was like a modern-day hippie, very unorganized, never cared what people thought of her, she stood up for what was right, no matter what, and could foresee the future of education and childcare in the district.

They saw something in me that I could not foresee, just as Pastor Freeman. Ms. Keys would tell me every time she saw me, "Don't stay here too long because I see great things for you in education." I would just smile and nod my head but thought, *Not in education*! Ms. Powers really showed me how to be an exceptional leader, journalist, educator, and communicator, working in the District of Columbia for childcare. She would give me the ins and outs of the government and would tell me to always keep my eyes and ears open. It did not take me long to heed what they all were saying. I just played the game and took lots of mental notes. I was only twenty-three when I started, so I had time to learn all of what I needed if I were to stay in DC and be successful. Maybe not in education, but I knew I would be a successful! When you strive to be a great leader, you must learn how to take the criticism with the blessings. Many call themselves a leader, but as they say, only a few are called. I believe I am one who has been called to lead people to successful futures through helping them where they seem to lack the push needed to succeed. This is most likely where my motherly nature came about that I never saw. Motherhood!

MOTHERHOOD

I usually don't get attached too easily, but that changed when I met you.

—Unknown Author

Mothers hold their children's hands for a while, but their hearts forever.

—Unknown Author

MOTHER

A mother's love comes in all different shapes, sizes, colors, and spirits. A mother is a symbolization for an expressed acronym like Mommy, Mom, Momma, Mama, or Ma.

When you become a mother, there are no instructions; you do what your mother did or some female influence in your family who represented themselves as to what a mother should do.

All mothers make mistakes: some are little and some are big, but no matter what your mother does, she does it because she loves you more than she loves herself and would do anything for you to have your basic needs met.

As children, we sometimes think our mothers could do better; but as we grow into adulthood or become mothers ourselves, we see what struggle a mother endures just to provide for her children.

So maybe mothers do not do everything right, but they do their best with what gift God has given them. No matter what, they are still your chosen mother who loves and adores you.

Now that I am a mother, I see traits of my mother, grandmother, sisters, and aunts in me when it comes to me being a mother. It's not an easy job, but it's a precious gift God gave to me to nurture, respect, and care for no matter what.

Mothers are beautiful flowers God put on this earth to make His precious buds that will someday grow into glorious plants who leave their leaves to keep growing and growing and growing.

So to all the mothers, whether biological, adopted, or otherwise (grandmother, aunt, sister, cousin, coach, mentor), are symbolizations of your mother whom you love, cherish, respect, adore, hug, kiss, and whatever else she asks because either she has or will do anything for you (no questions asked).

By LaShawn J. Tracy

My Mom

Now let's understand a little bit about my mom and our family role. We are a very close family who have been raised by a woman who is an introvert but very wise, clever, strict, loving, patient, passionate, protective, respectable, stressor, aggressive, God-fearing, has a power over all her children and grandchildren, and has very high expectations for everyone. She's not a woman who takes no lightly! She is a fighter, warrior, and very private lady! She expects for you to follow the gifts God has given to all of us. She meets no strangers and is loved by most. She gives more than she receives.

My mom has raised all her children with the understanding that education is important, which meant that she will get you through high school, but the rest is up to you. You get a choice to go on to college or go to work. If you do not want to do one of those, you must move out on your own. She doesn't close her door to anyone but expects greatness! She is very family-oriented and expects her children to teach their children that family comes first, no matter what. My mom, to say the least, is very intriguing!

My mom is the one whom we fear more than my fathers because her voice can make you crumble, even from a distance (crying like a baby). She has never cursed at any of her children or grandchildren and demands respect from everyone. She has never even called us out of our names (maybe each other's name [smile]). She doesn't like for anyone to talk about her babies (all of us are babies, no matter how old we are). There are nine children left here on earth, and we all have a piece of her instilled in us. My mom would move hell over high waters for her children and family. If she can help it, she is there no matter what!

My mom has raised us to the best of her ability because her mother died when she was six years old. She was raised by her father who gave her anything she wanted and taught her what he knew. I believe by her being raised by her father, she is very protective of the men in the family. She has created little spoiled, self-centered, self-indulged, and self-serving males, but the females are very independent, aggressive, arrogant, and tough. My mom taught the females to be just like her, and they do the same thing with their sons (interesting but a learned behavior). I did not pick up this behavior because I am tough on both of my children.

My mom has minor illnesses which she takes little to no medication. Most of her ailments come from being in an abusive marriage to her first husband. She hardly eats out and maintains a healthy diet. She eats out more now because it's only her and my father at home, but it's still not a lot. She is there whenever any of her children, grandchildren, nieces, nephews, cousins, etc. need her. My mom is the pillar of our family, and whatever she says, we do without question (I think I'm next in line huh?). So when it came to my turn to need her, just let's read what she and my family does for me.

MOTHERHOOD: PART 1

As I said previously, I never wanted to be a mommy, but God had other plans for me. See, God is always in control, we just think we control things (smiling). It took me some time to adjust to being someone's biological mommy. When I found out I was pregnant, I was shocked, confused, in denial, and upset. I was married, and all the right things were in place, but I did not want to have children. I even contemplated an abortion because I was not ready, and I did not think I would be a good mother. I knew days before I even said anything to Kelvin because I was in disbelief. So when the nurse called and said, "Congratulations, you are having a baby, do you want to keep it?" I hesitated. Kelvin on the other hand said *yes*!

I had helped raise my nephews when I was a teenager; had been a stepmom since 1999, and god-mommy/auntie since 1990 and 2000, but having children of your own is different. I helped Marilyn raise Tara, and everyone thought she was mine because she was always with me. I took her to work with me and did almost everything with her. She would call me Mommy Shawnee, then one day, she started calling me Awnie which has stuck (smiling). Tara has everyone calling me that until today (giggling).

It took me about seven months to bond with Kayla because I just couldn't believe I was pregnant and going to be a mommy. I did, however, do everything I was supposed to do to make sure I was going to have a happy healthy baby. I made sure I read to her, we talked to her through my belly music belt with microphone, and took my prenatal pills. I wore the belt around my belly from the beginning months to the end. I think that's why she loves music today! Everything an expecting mother is supposed to do, I did!

So as expected, when Kayla was born, Tara became another big sister/cousin to her. They did everything together and did not let anyone mess with the other, no matter who it was (smiling). It was

122

cute! However, Kayla needed to boss people around because she was always wanting to play, write, dance, or just be bossy. She acted a little like me (funny). Her dad spent a lot of time with her playing and things, but I was in school and working full-time so playing took up too much of my time on some occasions. I remember saying, "You need a brother or sister to be your friend." Not really saying I wanted another child, but I just wanted someone who could keep her company since her brother and sister were twelve and fourteen years older than her, and Tara did not live with us. It would just be easier if she had a little brother or sister.

Then in January, I passed out in Walmart and was taken to the hospital and was told I was pregnant. I thought, *Oh boy, Kayla is going to have a friend.* It was a pleasant feeling but also a little scary because now I was responsible for two of my own biological children who I would have to raise to be productive citizens and mold them into independent beings. *Oh, how will I do being a mother to my own children? Will I pass or fail? Can I really do this?* This would be my most challenging adventure for the rest of my life and only I could do it, but I would need the help of those before me. I would not be afraid to ask for help when I need it!

Tara is like a big sister/cousin to Kayla and Layden. But once I had my own children, I turned Tara over to her parents, and I continue to be a big part of her life. She will always be my baby too! However, it was time for me to be a full-time mommy to my own children which has been awesome because I can mold them a little. They are part of my genetics, so I have an opportunity to instill my morals and values on them, praying that they will continue to be respectful, caring, and loveable children.

After Layden was born, I took motherhood more seriously because now I had a daughter and a son to protect. I did not want anyone to be more of an influence on my children than me (selfish). However, I had no idea how to be a nurturing mother because I never showed emotion, and I wasn't the huggable one. I wanted all my children to know the meaning of love, so I put on a new hat which was going to be a challenge, but I was determined to do my best by my children. I began displaying my actions like I thought a loving mommy would act (my opinion). It wasn't an actual act, I was just trying to figure out how to be more emotional and nurturing. I just have to be myself, and that is nurturing enough because children can see the true you.

I saw and felt that all four (five if you include Tara) children needed to know that they had a mother who would do anything to make sure that they could lead healthy lives. I am very protective! I felt my hands were a little tied with the older two since they had both parents playing a major role in their lives, but I still made a point to leave part of my mark on them. Now that I was totally responsible for two little lives, I made a sacrifice to protect them from negative influences, keeping up with their education, and allowing them to have as stress-free-as-possible childhood. This was something I tried with the older two, but I just couldn't get the hold that I needed because I had a little fight from beyond my control. They knew I was there for them no matter what, even if I wasn't their biological parent. In spite of what others may have thought, I did not treat any of the children differently, I just had two I was more responsible for now. It makes a difference, even if it is not intentional because with your own children, you can push the limit; but with others, you may get a pushback from their parents.

I did not go anywhere that my children could not go with me unless it was work-related. I very seldom went out with friends or anything. I am blessed to have had plenty of family support which I needed because I did work a lot, especially with Kayla, but not so much with Layden. I had gained a new characteristic once Layden was born—charisma. I was determined to renew my personality so I could be a blessing to my children. Little did I know, though, I would be diagnosed with leukemia a year after Layden was born. Let's see how I handle motherhood then!

BIBLIOGRAPHY

Encyclopedia of Children's Health. "Birth Order." (2015). www.healthofchildren.com/B/Birth-Order.html.

Faith. merriam-webster.com. (2015). https://www.merriam-webster.com/dictionary/faith.

Glaucoma Foundation. (2015). Glaucoma. https://glaucomafoundation.org/.

Mature. merriam-webster.com. (2015). http://www.merriam-webster.com/dictionary/mature.

Sivananda, Swami. "This is the Secret of Success." (2015). http://www.nobelthoughts.com/2015/07/19/this-is-the-secret-of-success-swami-sivananda/.

Scott, Stuart. EPSY Speech. (2014). https://genius.com/Stuart-scott-2014-espys-speech-annotated.

Wikipedia. (2015). Griffin. https://en.wikipedia.org/wiki/Griffin.

To Be Continued
In
Book 2
Fortitude Taught Me

Fortitude Taught Me

Treatment, Testimony, Team, Task, Talent, Thrive, Trust

CONTENTS

PREFACE

When I originally started thinking about writing a book about my life, I did not think I had much to offer. As a human, we take many things that happen in our lives for granted because we don't fully understand what has been placed before us and who is actually in control. We assume we make our own decisions and our own choices, but they were preplanned before we were even thought of becoming part of the ultimate plan. No matter what you believe, there is no way we can live on this earth without guidance of some sort.

Now don't get me wrong, you have the ability to make your own decisions because we have freedom of will; but with that freedom comes consequences—good and bad. I am a living testimony of that factor. No, my life has not been as challenging as some, but for me, my challenges are all I can handle, and for me, they are significant.

I am not here to judge anyone! I am just trying to make sure we all understand that we make choices that we sometimes must live through in order to find relief or justifications. Justifications for our actions are tough for a lot of us, but we have to go through them for a reason and finally understand why we had to do the things we chose.

My books are just that—a testimony to what I have been through in my journey through life. I have not been through what I have seen in my life others have gone through and succeeded or even failed, but I can say I challenge all of you to read my story; make a judgment for yourself, then use my story as a guide for you to keep pressing on because at the end of the day, it's just you who is looking through that mirror, seeing your reflection on the other side. No one can tell you what you are going through but you. There is help out there that can help you manage your life, but *you* and only *you* can change, alter, or make life what you want it to look like if you are willing to challenge yourself. It is a major step that even the best think they may not have to do, but believe me, we all must take that step; it's just up to you how long you are going to wait!

My editorial is ultimately different than ones you will ever see because I believe in challenge. I speak directly from my heart, and no one can challenge how I feel, my opinions, my interpretations, but not my feelings. That's my challenge to you after you have read my book; take a good look in the mirror, no matter what age you are, and set goals for yourself—some realistic and some you think may be unrealistic. Then challenge yourself to the quest that you will someday make these things happen. You don't have to write them down for others to see, just hold them in your heart and believe in yourself. Speak volume to your life, and you will see that, no matter how many books you read and stories about others you may come across. Remember, your legend is always the best because it belongs to you and no one else. Believe in the gifts and talents you have been given, big or small, just believe and dream! It will come true!

Resurrecting Through Grace and Mercy

Teach me to feel another's woe, to hide the fault I see,
that mercy I to others show, that mercy show to me.

—Alexander Pope

Grace

When I think of all the trials and tribulations that I have been through in my life, it's nothing but grace and mercy that keeps me steadfast. I have my times when I don't believe I deserve God's grace and mercy, but I believe Jesus did on the cross so I can be forgiven for the things in my life I will do that is not pleasing to His sight. However, I always try my best to treat others the way in which I want to be treated, and that is with respect. I believe respect is the ultimate sacrifice we make as humans on this earth because without it, the world is a disaster; and our ancestors fought and died for respect for themselves and others.

According to *Merriam-Webster Dictionary* (2016):

> *A simple definition is a way of moving that is smooth and attractive and that is not stiff or awkward; a controlled, polite, and pleasant way of behaving; and skills that are needed for behaving in a polite way in social situations. The full definition is unmerited divine assistance given humans for their regeneration or sanctification; a virtue coming from God; a state of sanctification enjoyed through divine grace; approval, favor -stayed in his good graces, archaic: mercy, pardon—a special*

favor: privilege—*each in his place, by right, not grace, shall rule his heritage—Rudyard Kipling; disposition to or an act or instance of kindness, courtesy, or clemency; a temporary exemption;* reprieve; *a charming or attractive trait or characteristic; a pleasing appearance or effect;* charm—*all the grace of youth—John Buchan; ease and suppleness of movement or bearing; used as a title of address or reference for a duke, a duchess, or an archbishop; a short prayer at a meal asking a blessing or giving thanks; plural capitalized; three sister goddesses in Greek mythology who are the givers of charm and beauty; a musical trill, turn, or appoggiatura; sense of propriety or right—had the grace not to run for elective office—Calvin Trillin; and the quality or state of being considerate or thoughtful.*

Mercy

Your grace and mercy have brought me through; I am living this moment because of you, your grace and mercy has given me the opportunities to reach for the things that would seem untouchable. Your grace and mercy have been my driving force to keep hope alive in the midst of all storms, adversities, and missions. When mercy has provided me with the compassion, forgiveness, motivation, and blessings to keep pushing, it can only be through my faith that I can excel. *Mercy* is a word that isn't used a lot because I believe it is misunderstood. When you ask for mercy, that means you want others to feel empathetic for you.

According to some definitions, *mercy is "kindness or help given to people who are in a very bad or desperate situation; a kind or forgiving treatment of someone who could be treated harshly; compassion or forgiveness shown towards someone whom it is within one's power to punish or harm; an event to be grateful for, especially because its occurrence prevents something unpleasant or provides relief from suffering."*

To fulfill life's journey, we must have mercy for others no matter the race, creed, ethnicity, disability, sex, gender, or belief. Mercy is not something we can live without!

GRIEF

You might be wondering why I would address grief when referring to grace and mercy. It is because sometimes, grief must happen for some people to experience or understand grace or mercy. Grief has many facets to it because it covers such a wide variety of losses and an almost unlimited range of emotions. Grief is not always a loss because of death; it could be emotions for the end of or change in a familiar pattern or behavior. Grief is not easy to articulate if you do not know how to express yourself through words. Some of us our grieving as you are reading this and don't even know it or why. We have been taught that there are seven stages of grief, and you must go through them simultaneously. However, these stages can occur at many different stages, depending on what you are grieving for. Here is the final model of grief: *"shock & denial; pain & guilt; anger & bargaining; "depression", reflection, loneliness; the upward turn; reconstruction & working through; and acceptance & hope"* (Recover-from-grief. com 2017).

If you have gone through or are still struggling with grief, please reach out to a friend, family, counselor, therapist, or someone with a listening ear. Please do not continue feeling this way without seeking help. There are many resources to help guide you with these stages and understanding that there is faith in His grace and mercy.

This leads me to my next section, "Becoming as One in the Eyes of God." We must spend our life with someone who makes us happy and that we can have compassion and forgiveness toward in all times.

BECOMING AS ONE IN
THE EYES OF GOD

*Spend your life with who makes you happy,
not with who you have to impress.*

—Unknown

B ecoming one in the eyes of the Lord is a special moment in anyone's life. This is supposed to be the time that you marry your best friend, lover, spiritual partner, and soul mate. For each marriage/relationship, there are always going to be challenges because you are two unique individuals who are trying to form a bond of one. Well, it was a little different for me. I had been with Kelvin for five years before we got married in June 2002. We had our ups and downs, but I never really thought of him as my best friend, soul mate, or confidant. I tried but there were some things that was preventing me from really trusting him. It could have been him throwing things back in my face when he had the opportunity, or me knowing that our relationship should have been seasonal, not permanent (shaking my head).

Once I got married in 2002, I had to start looking at life differently because now I had more responsibilities, and I had no choice but to grow up. I was always mature for my age, but now I had to really put it into action. I completed my master's degree in May 2003 and purchased our home in June 2003. In September 2003, I found out I was pregnant, and now this was really setting me back. Now I had another person I was responsible to care for which made me nervous and uneasy. Sharon and Shayna were the two who were not as happy with this situation. Sharon because she knew what I would have to go through, and Shayna because now I wasn't her role model once I had a child because that was never in my future. I just said God has foreseen something different for my future, and I wasn't in control. God will humble you when He needs to, and maybe that's what I needed at the time. I just follow His Word! This was when I realized that your life is already preselected, and it just depends on what road you take and if God planned that for you or not.

When I got married, I went back to Pennsylvania and many of my friends, coworkers, and family attended the wedding. I did not invite anyone from there because most of the people I talked to were men, and they were friends with Michael whom I thought I might still have strong feelings. He would not have wanted my friends from Pennsylvania there anyway because he was a little insecure when it came to my hometown. I was surprised when he agreed to have the wedding there, but it was cheaper than Maryland, DC, or Virginia.

My theme was Cinderella because I had the evil half-sisters (smiling)! My sisters are not evil, just a little aggressive (laughing). I wanted something that no one else ever tried, so all my wedding party walked in alone; the men walked in first from the front, and the ladies walked down the aisle. I followed by walking down the aisle in this form-fitting gown with a long train and glass slipper heels just like in the story of Cinderella (except the big dress which I was too short to be wearing). I knew no one would have expected me to wear such a form-fitting gown (smiling). My dad walked me down the aisle, and in my mind, I had so many doubts. My head was spinning because I knew I had second-guessed myself and let my family talk me into a situation I was not ready to partake. The whole time, I thought about calling it off, but I thought this was God's will in my mind but not in my heart. My dad kept saying I was just nervous! Anyone who know me knows that I rarely get nervous about things I feel are not right. However, I just went through with the ceremony, wishing I had made the right decision. I believed it was what God wanted, even if I questioned it. My wedding was the Richardson-Tracy family reunion as well for that year which we usually had in late July or early August. So we had a lot of people in attendance, about three hundred to be exact.

We have been hosting Richardson-Tracy family reunions since 1981. My mom and aunt Bunny started it in my parents' yard. Then in 2001, I guess the torch was passed to the children (mostly my siblings). After I had put a reunion together alone in 2004, when I had my first child as well, the torch was passed to me. Now everyone looks to me for advice for the reunions. I guess I have that leadership role I took from my mom. Ever since, I have always been in a leadership role.

Even though we were together for five years before we got married, I never investigated the signs. Please allow me to fill you in on why I believe there were early signs I wasn't supposed to get married to him. First, my wedding started late, and the clock was going up, not down (for those who are superstitious). Next, I twisted my ankle at the wedding reception, preventing me from staying until the end because it swelled up. Then he lost his job when we returned from the wedding and was involved in some legal problems from it. This incident was very strange because his employer and her family drove to Pennsylvania to witness the wedding, then fired him upon his return (confusing). We got it expunged but just to have gone through that was mind-blowing. Then he had such a hard time with group home jobs for some reason. I couldn't understand what was happening. It could have been he wanted in an industry that needed a degree. So I asked him to think about, maybe, changing his career or even opening a facility himself since he had all the expertise and loved working with troubled teen boys and coaching. Once we tried and he wasn't really putting forth the effort to open his own establishment, I just went with it and continued with what I wanted for my future. We had very different dreams and goals (first sign of destruction, not being equally yoked)!

After we got married, we moved in with Pops (his dad) so we could save money to buy a home instead of renting. We lived with him for about eight to ten months before finding the perfect home. We could not have lived with him much longer because he was a chain-smoker, and I kept getting sick from the smoke. At that time, I was trying to work more than I was home to prevent me from possibly becoming very ill and looking for a place to move. Once we met Ann from Remax, the process moved a lot faster.

Sidenote: I believe I am related to Ann's ex-husband who is a Richardson, my mom's relative. I just can't prove it right now. So on June 30, 2003, we closed on our first home. After a long search, we finally found somewhere we could call our own. Our thoughts, at first, were to find a starter house and, in a few years, move to a location we would retire. As life had it, we got comfortable in the neighborhood and did not want to move. It was a great choice, I think! Since we both grew up in communities and neighborhoods were everyone knew everyone, we saw it was only fit for us to do it for our children. In addition, the age range in the community varied which gave us a better advantage to stay. The home had three bedrooms, a finished basement with a bedroom, one and a half baths, a full backyard with potential, a built-in grill and shed. It was just what we needed at the time. We had two children who would have their own bedrooms. It was perfect! My family would not have a hard time visiting because it was right off the highway. That was a big thing with me, finding the right home! I loved it!

On September 10, 2003, I found out I was pregnant. I was devastated because I did not want any children, plus I wanted to continue with my doctorate degree in counseling or clinical psychology. However, I had to put that on hold. Some family members were happy for me, and others felt like I did. It took me almost six months to really accept the pregnancy. However, I made sure I did everything right so that I would have a healthy baby. I bought all the current technology that would help with healthy brain development and bonding. We decided we did not want to know the sex of the baby because I wanted it to be a surprise since it was my first child. However, during my second trimester, they told me that the baby was breeched, and I would more than likely have to have a C-section. No, no, no! First, I'm having a baby, and now you want to cut me. I was not ready for that! I ended up having three procedures called external cephalic version.

According to familydoctor.org (2015), *"External cephalic version is a way to try to turn a baby from breech position to head-down position while it's still in the mother's uterus. In other words, external cephalic version means turning the baby from outside of the abdomen so that it's in the head-down position. Your doctor will use his or her hands on the outside of your abdomen to try to turn the baby."*

This did not work because the more they pushed, the more the baby pushed back. Meanwhile I had this procedure done three times because I was determined not to have to get cut. So I had to have a Cesarean delivery which I did not want at all because she couldn't move. This put me into depression because now I had to have this ugly cut on my stomach. On June 20, 2004 (Father's Day), I gave birth to a baby girl, Kayla, at 7:13 a.m., at Holy Cross Hospital in Silver Spring, Maryland. This was Kelvin's, my father's (his first biological grandchild), and Pop-Pop's gift! The doctor did a very good job on my delivery and with my cut. However, we were told that Kayla could possibly have problems with her right hip because she was sitting on her leg and that we would have to massage and stretch it out. Kayla wasn't having it! She stretched out her own leg and drank a half-bottle of milk and two bottles of water. My baby was dehydrated having all that pressure on her (smile)! We did see a tiny cut on her butt where the doctor had to cut, so we called it her birthmark. She still has it today but the taller she gets, the further up her back it goes (smile).

After the doctor told us we may have to exercise her leg, she showed the nurse she was not going to have anyone help her with her leg, and her hip was good. She stretched it out, and she hasn't had a problem with it at all. We had a healthy 7 lbs. 4 oz. and 22 1/2 in. long healthy little girl with straight black hair and ten fingers and toes. She was my world now. Kayla was so much like me already, not wanting any help (independent). Funny thing was we thought we were being creative with her name by naming her after us, but we were fooled because that name is so popular; it was original for us anyways. I took a year off work to bond with her. I worked from home after my sixth-month checkup. She was our first child together, and he was a great father to her. Kayla was his world! Even though he had two older children, Kayla was the baby.

After Kayla turned one year old, we agreed that we needed another family car. So he was supposed to purchase a family car because she needed to be in a car seat, Bria, and Bryan who was 6'3". I had a five-passenger SUV truck. He still needed a car we all could ride in as a family. He went out and bought a two-door convertible

BMW. I was very, very angry because that was selfish, and he had a family of five. Then he said that a baby car seat couldn't go in the car because it would tear up the seats. I said it many, many times, "Why did you buy it then? You are a married man with three children?" I immediately wanted out of this marriage because he was selfish, and it wasn't going to get any better. I am family-oriented, and he is selfish (sign 2)!

Now how do you get out of something you stood before God and said you would be there through anything? I was stuck with a man I lost all the love I had because we were of two different worlds. I never forgave him! I called it his selfish ass car and wanted no part of it. I said he better kept that car until the wheels fell off because I was done. Why should I have to put up with such selfishness? Oh, I want out! However, how do you make this decision when you stood before God and witnesses saying that you would stay together forever in addition to now having a family of your own? My, my, my!

However, I went back to work full-time in June 2005. This was a brand-new challenge for me: raising my own child, two stepchildren who were teenagers, Bryan and Bria; helping my sister with my four-year-old niece/goddaughter, Tara; a husband, working as a director full-time; and writing grants. It seemed like a lot, but I handled it! Since my stepchildren were twelve and fourteen years older than Kayla, plus she was so grown at an early age, I felt her having a friend to play with would be good for her and I. He and Marilyn spent most of the time with Kayla when I went back to work because she was too young to attend my center. However, once she turned two, she was my rode dog. She was very shy and did not like men, especially Pop-Pop. Every time he would try to pick her up, she would scream her head off. Kayla did this until she was about two years old, then she loved him. However, she went to my dad, but she knew when he had been tasting, and her eyes would get big, never crying, saying, "Please don't try to pick me up" (laughing). She just really didn't take to too many people (acting like me). She did not trust men at all (big eyes)! Kayla is loved by everyone who meets her. I thought it was just because I never wanted children and she was the first, but she is just a loving child. She would do anything to help, and she held conversations as though she was an adult already (observant). Kayla started walking, singing, and snapping her fingers at eight months (Easter 2005, also her aunt Sharon's birthday). She hasn't stopped since! One thing about Kayla, she is just very moody (one minute talking, the next not wanting to be bothered).

During this time, I really noticed that Kayla needed a friend because she wanted all of my time and attention, but I was struggling giving into her, working full-time, going to school full-time, helping raise teenagers, and maintaining a household. It was becoming overwhelming to say the least. I managed, but I was tired emotionally. I never considered having another child, but I thought it could be a plus too for Kayla.

In 2006, I started working on my own business because I wanted to venture out in the childcare field and help people open centers in DC. When I knew I could not work under anyone anymore, it was time to start my own business. Although by this time I oversaw the center, it still belonged to the church. I had given the center my five-plus years, and it was time for me to grow out. Yes, I can get bored with a job if I know I have put my all into it, and I'm not growing. I started as a technical assistant consultant for myself. He and I tried opening a lawn-and-garden business, but I thought it was a bad idea because we would only be working about five months out of the year. We did try it to see what would happen, but since I didn't help much, it fell through. He really loved working with at-risk teens, so we attended the orientation to start a group home for boys under Kayla's name, but that fell through because he did not want to go through with it at the time because of the changes to the group homes. He really didn't like to challenge himself when it came to business; he left it all up to me, and I didn't feel it was my dream, so I would just help.

I encouraged him to go back to school to seek his degree so he could fully run the group homes and be the football coach he dreamed about becoming someday. However, he started that and did not finish because of academia at UDC. I tried to encourage him to go to Prince George's Community College because it was an in-state school, and he had to basically start over anyways because he had been out of school so long (stressor). Kelvin decided he did not want to pursue his degree, so I kept growing with my own entrepreneurship, and he continued being an assistant coach at McNamara High School, District Heights, Maryland. I never stopped him from striving for his dream, it was just taking a lot of my energy because he had other things he wanted to do, I guess. This was when I knew I was fighting silently within my soul.

On January 10, 2007, I found out I was pregnant with my second child after passing out in Walmart, Clinton, Maryland. I was determined to have a different outlook on this pregnancy because I was now thirty-two, and the risk of high pregnancy are more common after thirty. I did not let anything bother me. I was happy, outgoing, pleasant, and stress-free the entire pregnancy because I did not want an unhealthy baby. I wanted another one who acted like me (smiling).

When we found out I was pregnant, I was relieved, but he was very unhappy because he was done having children in his mind. He would say things to me that were very hurtful, but I would just smile and kept a cheerful spirit so that negativity would not get to my baby. He loved Kayla, and that was all he wanted. He made it clear that three children were all he wanted. However, we were married, so in my eyes, another child would be helpful for him, Kayla, and me. This was when true colors started to show (sign)! He had accused me of cheating on him and that our son wasn't his. He would say the most horrible things to me the entire pregnancy and barely even went with me to the doctor's appointments (not a best friend). I just considered that this would be my baby, and he would have nothing to worry about. When I found out it was a boy, I just thought he would change his mind about him, but he didn't. He kept saying he was my child, and Kayla was more his child. They were both my children no matter what, and I was not going to let his bad energy influence them in any way because I knew how it would end. I did what I had to do to make sure my babies were loved unconditionally by me, especially my son because I was already showing Kayla the way I knew how. I did not treat my children any different, but their father did.

I did not want to know the gender, but Layden was proud to let us see who he was during our first ultrasound. He was not shy! My C-section was scheduled for October 22, 2007, but my water broke on Saturday, October 13, 2007, at 1:30 a.m., while I was writing my term paper for my psychology class that was due Sunday by midnight. I had to complete that before I could go to the hospital, plus when I called, the nurse did not seem very concerned since I was not having any contractions.

Once I arrived at the hospital and checked in, the doctor gave me a choice of a vaginal birth or C-section. I asked what was better. She stated that vaginal is always the perfect choice, but I could be in labor for forty-eight hours since I had not dilated yet. Oh, I could not have that much pressure on me, so I agreed to the C-section. Yes, it would be my second C-section, but I wasn't planning on having any more! I delivered my baby boy, Layden, at 4:10 a.m., at Holy Cross Hospital in Silver Spring, Maryland, at six pounds, eight ounces, twenty-one inches long. I picked out his name because I wanted him to have the same initials as I since his dad really didn't want him. So I picked a name I knew would be original, and yes, there are no other Laydens. He was born with jaundice and had to be monitored before we could leave the hospital. He looked just like me and my father. Everyone would tease, saying he looked like a Saudi Arabian child because he had straight jet-black hair, and it was all over him. He was surely my son (hairy!). He has such a beautiful smile that will lighten up your day.

Now I had two children who were my pride and joy. Who could have asked for anything better, a girl and a boy? Our family consisted of a firstborn boy and a last born boy with two girls in the middle. The boys are the girls' protectors! I figured my family was complete. No, it wasn't perfect on the inside, but from the outside looking in, everything was great. I had been through so much, but I would always keep it to myself because it was the life I chose, and I had to work it out the best way I knew how. Plus I did not have time for opinions or suggestions because in some way, I was angry because I felt my family knew I never wanted to be in this situation, *ever*. I just had to believe God saw things in another light.

He did not have a relationship with Layden until I got sick, and he had no choice. If you ask him, he says he had a great relationship with Layden. Although Layden acts just like me (laughing)! Funny thing, Kayla has my characteristics and personality I had as a child, and Layden has my characteristics and personality as an adult. Just think of it as a lot to handle and very hard to understand!

One day, I was watching Tyler Perry's movie *Why Did I Get Married Too?*, and the character played by Janet Jackson said to the other women that you know if you love someone and want to work it out if you write down the pros and cons. If the pros outweigh the cons, then you belong together. So I did it! Let me say, it wasn't all bad, but the bad outweighed the good in this marriage. I am younger than him but much more mature when it comes to many things. As I said before, I have an ole soul, not to be reckoned with. I felt he never really knew me which made everything difficult, but I will say that it probably was my fault because I didn't want him to know me after the 2005 selfish act. Then I started seeing more and more selfish things he would do that really got under my skin (I just kept it to myself and smiled). In some sense, I think this wasn't meant to be from the start. We should have just remained friends and no further than a true friendship. Now I don't even want to be bothered with him unless it has to do with the children, and that is limited!

As a little girl, I always said I never wanted to get married or have children because it was too much of a responsibility that I see others fail at or was just very unhappy, and I did not want to experience any of them. However, since my family had a way of making me think I should do certain things because it's the right thing to do, I went on and got married. Something wasn't right, though!

On December 8, 2008, I was diagnosed with acute myelogenous leukemia (AML) the doctors told me that since AML was such a progressive form of leukemia that my life expectancy would only be about two years. It's interesting how things change when God steps in! On December 8, 2008, I was diagnosed with acute myelogenous leukemia (AML). The doctors told me that since AML was such a progressive form of leukemia that my life expectancy would only be about two years. I was diagnosed with cancer of the blood which was very rare in African American woman and even rarer for individuals in their thirties. I was gracious that it had a curable rate of three years, which meant God was trying to tell me something. I believe it was to get out of my marriage, but I couldn't figure out how he expected me to do that with two children who adored their father. In addition, I never wanted to have my children raised in a two-family household because I grew up with both parents in the same home. All I could really think about was how great my God is! My original two-year death sentence changed immediately to a three-year success story. This is how quickly God works! I would be able to enjoy raising my children since Kayla was four years old, and Layden was only fourteen months old. I just kept saying, "God gave this to me for a reason, and I'm going to see it through. I don't know what is in store for me, but I know it is something good!" I was going to follow His Word and have the Holy Spirit take over my body for His work to be done. Thank you, God, for all you have done for me! Let's talk about these hospital stays during this diagnosis!

HOSPITAL STAYS

PRINCE GEORGE'S HOSPITAL CENTER STAY

On Monday, December 8, 2008, Ms. Roxanne, Kelvin's mom, took me to the hospital. When we got there, I was too weak to walk, so they pushed me in a wheelchair. We were sitting in the waiting room, waiting for the doctor to call to have me sent to a room. We sat there from approximately 4:15 p.m. until 5:30 p.m., waiting. She was so frustrated she called her doctor again, and he said that he had called over an hour ago and told them my name was Michelle (wrong). So the doctor called back, and they had us go through registration in order to get to the room. I remember myself just asking everyone to repeat themselves because I was getting delusional. After a minute, Ms. Roxanne started answering for me because I just couldn't think anymore. I'm glad she was there with me, and I *thank* her for everything!

When I got to the room, the nurses immediately started an intravenous access (IV), poking, drawing blood, giving me fluids, and running lots of test. It seemed like they were taking blood every hour on the hour. The doctor wanted to do a colonoscopy. I had thought my throat was too dry, so how were they going to do that because they can't go through my rectum because of the bleeding (shaking my head)? So I asked the nurse if I had to agree to it because it could tear my esophagus. She told me that I could deny any service I wanted. Well, I did deny that one and said they would have to figure something else out because I was too dehydrated. So many tests were taken, but the initial test all came back negative.

Ms. Roxanne stayed with me until Kelvin got there around 9:00 p.m. The children were over at Marilyn's, so they were okay for the night. He stayed and fell asleep in the next bed, but the nurses came in and told him he couldn't lie there. He stayed all night or until they told him he had to leave. There was nothing happening that night but them drawing blood, so it was okay for him to leave and come back in the morning. He did get there about 10:00 a.m., but if that was me, he would have wanted me there at 8:00 a.m. when visiting hours started, no question (how I was fooled).

They were priming and poking me all night, trying to figure out where the bleeding was coming from. They could not stop it because every time I would go to the bathroom, the toilet would be full of blood. They even had me put a pad down on the bed just in case I started bleeding. They were so confused they put a measuring bowl in the toilet to see if they could tell how much I was bleeding, but it would just overflow every time. This was getting scary now because I knew I was losing too much blood. I stayed awake because all I could think about was bleeding out in my sleep and not waking up to see my babies. So I just watched TV all night, praying that God would take care of me.

On December 9, 2008, the doctor had come in and said that I was going to need a blood transfusion because I was losing too much blood. However, before receiving the transfusion, they told me the consequences, along with Kelvin and Pastor Briggs. He did not want me to get it because of the risk, but I had no choice—get it or die. I was too young to die, and I needed to be here for my babies. It was a no-brainer for me (smile). The doctor assured us that the chances of the blood being tainted was slim to none because they test the blood several times before releasing it. If it were ten to twenty years prior, then I may have had to be cautious, but not in today's time.

So I had my first blood transfusion around 2:00 p.m. on December 9, 2008. This was the nastiest tasting thing I had ever experienced besides liver and Brussel sprouts. Just think, the blood was being transfused through my IV, and I could taste it (frown).

However, I could feel myself getting stronger and not hurting as bad. My migraine even started to go away, but the bleeding continued. I kept thinking what this could be because my body was really out of control right now. It seemed like the more blood I received, the more I was losing in the toilet. This was frustrating and frightening all at the same time. The good part was I was in the room by myself, so I didn't have to be bothered with another person's issue. In addition, I could run back and forth to the bathroom as I pleased. Which was almost every fifteen to twenty minutes! If I felt my stomach acting funny, I went to the bathroom (smiling). I was not going to take that chance of seeing blood on the bed because I knew I would pass out. I could not stomach any blood, vomit, slobber, or anything that was not normal. My stomach was weak when it came to sickness (frowning).

Later that day, he had brought the children to see me. I was so excited! Kayla was asking me what was wrong, and I told her I did not know, that the doctors were still trying to find out. Layden was acting like he feared me and wouldn't come to me. This was just heartbreaking, to say the least, because I never wanted my children to feel like they didn't know me. Layden knew it was me, but he would just stare at me. I guess in his mind, he thought, *I just saw my mommy, and she did not have all these things hooked to her.* They were my inspiration to battle whatever this was that had overtaken my body, but after that day, I became even more persistent to fight. Satan, take a back seat because you are not winning this one! My babies need their mommy, and I will do all that I can to see this come true with the help of my Father in heaven.

On Wednesday, December 10, 2008, was when they gave me the diagnosis that I either had AML or a serious vitamin-B12 deficiency. As you will read later, you will see what I was thinking (smile). The doctor told me that I was going to be transported to either Johns Hopkins Hospital or the University of Maryland Medical Center in Baltimore for further treatment. I chose the closest to the highway so my family could find me easily. I had been at Prince George's Community Hospital for only three days, and my arms looked like I was on drugs because of all the black marks from the blood being drawn. It did not look appealing at all! I had to go to another hospital with these marks on my arms (disturbed.) The only good thing I can say about this stay was that I had a room to myself, which is unusual for a community hospital, and they think they found out what was wrong with me.

However, right before I was being transferred, a woman with kidney disease and something else was admitted as my roommate. All she kept doing was hollering and screaming about her itching and needing medicine. She stripped all her clothes off and was just lying in the bed, naked (horrific sight). I had visitors come in, and she was just lying there, without covering up, and her curtain not closed all the way, just naked and hollering. What a sight we got that night (smiling)! We tried keeping the curtain closed and I tried to ignore her, but the EMS was not coming fast enough to transport me. It got so bad that after everyone left around 7:30 p.m., I started feeling sorry for her, so I started talking to her, trying to keep her mind off the itching. We talked about anything and everything just to get her from hollering. I don't even think I got up to use the bathroom after everyone left because she was doing so much hollering (laughing). I can say it worked until 10:00 p.m., right before the transportation came for me. She went on and on until the nurse finally gave her something to put her to sleep. What a blessing!

When the EMS got there, I was so glad because that lady was driving me crazy, plus I had to keep walking past her side of the room to get to the bathroom. I even tried to hold it, but I was getting nervous because they couldn't stop the bleeding. I didn't know the side effects, and I could have made it worse by holding it, so I just dealt with her naked peripheral sight I was getting when I walked past (shaking my head every time). She had no shame, though!

Around 10:30 p.m., PG nursing staff removed my IV because they said I couldn't travel with their hospital's IV to another hospital. It did not make any sense to me since I was going to need it when I got to the other hospital, but I just went with their policy. The transportation service had arrived to transfer me to the University of Maryland Medical Center but on the bone marrow transplant side because that was the only room available. They asked me about my

IV, and I told them that the nurse informed me that I could not go to another hospital with their IV in my arm. They just shook their heads in denial. I was wondering about me getting liquids (shrugging shoulders). Marilyn had called before I left and said she would meet me at the hospital because she was coming from bingo in Laurel, and it wasn't that far. I had to deny it because she is very emotional, and I was not prepared for that right then. I did thank her for the gesture, though.

UMMC Hospital Stay

When I arrived at UMMC, my nurse was Birney, and my tech nurse was Jackie. They had assisted me on settling in and gave me instructions about what was going to happen that day so I could be prepared. Birney had to start me another IV because I needed fluids. However, I still couldn't eat, drink, nor have ice cubes. My mouth was as dry as a desert on cotton! But they kept saying I couldn't have anything. This was abuse, I thought! I knew it was just protocol since they didn't really know the test I would need to determine what cancer I had and how it needs to be treated. I was extraordinarily dry! Since I knew what was happening, I tried to get some sleep but was only taking naps. Birney gave me some Ativan to help me sleep since I hadn't slept in three days, worrying about what was going on with my thirty-four-year-old body. I just kept thinking, *I just had a baby last year, and they didn't notice any abnormality in my blood. Weird!* So I fell asleep for what I thought was four or five hours, but it was only about a half-hour. I could not sleep for anything!

Around 8:00 a.m., my telephone rang, and it's my brother Evan, calling, asking me why I was not listed at the hospital and that he needed my room number. Well, I had no idea why I wasn't listed, but I gave him my room number, which was 1036, I think. To my surprise, he, his fiancé (now wife), and my nephew/godson, Kent, came walking through the door. They all looked nervous, like they didn't know what they were going to see when they walked in, but I looked like myself, so no worries there. They still left looking worried! He lives in Philadelphia, Pennsylvania, so it only took him about an hour to make it to the hospital. They stayed until the team of doctors came in to talk to me about what I would be going through the next few hours and days. The doctor said it was going to be very intense and that I would have to go through chemotherapy. I had to stay in the hospital for a while so they could stop the bleeding, and I would need some blood, platelets, and plasma. When my brother left, he looked very worried but wasn't saying too much.

A few hours later, my mom, dad, and Kelvin showed up. It seemed like they showed up right in time for my first round of treatments. First, I had my bone marrow biopsy. Now I had asked the doctor before this procedure how it felt, and he said, "Some people say it's like having a baby." So that's what I was thinking. Oh, hell no! So, the fellow had told me not to move because it was not going to take that long. No! No! No! Not only did it take long, but it was the worst pain I had ever felt in my life (crying profusely). Then, the fellow could not get the tool to cut through my bone to even get to my bone marrow. Let me tell you that they were going through my right hip bone to get the bone marrow. They tried numbing my skin, but that did not work. He tried three times before he sent for another doctor. I told them if they couldn't get it this time that they would have to figure out another way. So the main bone marrow resident doctor finally got in and sucked out some of my bone marrow to be tested. Now I am a person who usually has a high tolerance for pain, but this procedure was so, so painful that I wouldn't wish it on my worst enemy (which I don't think I have any). I was crying so bad that when the fellow couldn't get in and the other doctor came in, he tried to console me while the other doctor was doing the procedure. My bones were so hard they had the hardest time trying to succeed at the biopsy. My bones being this hard is not normal for leukemia patients, but mine were and were not getting weak or fragile.

The procedure consisted of me lying on my side in a fetal position with a pillow between my knees and a pillow in my arms.

As seen above, the instruments are used for performing tissue biopsies with a single tissue penetration. The elongated instrument comprises a hollow aspirating needle for aspirating bone marrow fluid, a hollow biopsy needle telescoped within the aspirating needle, and a solid stylet removable telescope within the biopsy needle, all of which coaxially fit together. The stylet comprises a sharp distal end extending outward from the biopsy needle for initially penetrating body tissue and occluding the interior of the biopsy needle. The biopsy needle comprises a distal end normally projecting from the aspirating needle for thereafter, penetrating a bone and obtaining a solid bone marrow sample. The bulbous biopsy needle's distal end is sharpened for captivating a specimen. It has a pair of relief slots, dividing it into bulbous halves, that are compressed together when the needle coaxially moves through the aspirating needle after withdrawal from tissue.

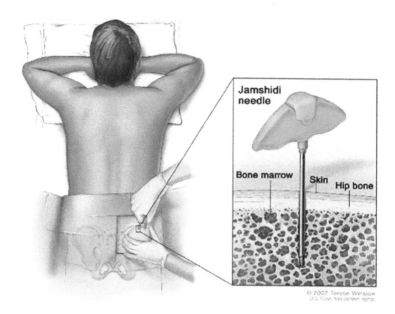

Jamshidi needle

Bone marrow | Skin | Hip bone

© 2007 Terese Winslow
U.S. Govt. has certain rights

In operation, the instrument is first inserted through the skin and muscle tissue to the bone surface. The stylet is then withdrawn. As the instrument subsequently penetrates the cortical bone and enters the bone marrow cavity, the biopsy needle fills with a tissue sample. The biopsy sample is captivated by compression of the bulbous portion as that needle segment is removed. Afterward the outer aspirating needle that remains in place in the bone is suctioned by an attachable syringe, and liquid bone marrow from the marrow cavity is aspirated into the syringe (Google search 2015). After they finished, I told them not to tell anyone else this procedure was like having a baby because it is ten times worse, and I never even had a vaginal birth, but I knew it wasn't this bad.

When the fellow went out into the waiting room to get my family, he told them that I would not stop crying. So when they came in, I was lying straight up and down, crying my eyes out, and my mom said, "The doctor told us you wouldn't stop crying." They said that must have been painful because I don't cry and can withstand pain.

I told them that I never wanted that procedure again because I don't think I can take that pain awake. It was pure agony!

Next I received a PICC line:

> *A peripherally inserted central catheter, often called a "PICC line," is a long, very thin, flexible tube that is usually placed into one of the large veins in the arm, often just above or just below the elbow. This tube is threaded into a large vein above the right side of the heart* (in my right arm).

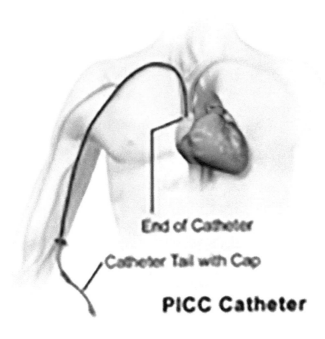

End of Catheter

Catheter Tail with Cap

PICC Catheter

> *The PICC line will be used to give IV (intravenous) medicines or fluids. Because the tube is so small and flexible, the line can last several weeks to months, which means fewer needle pokes and less pain. The PICC line can be flushed and capped off when not in use. When it is time to give medicine,*

*the medicine is connected to the PICC line and dis-
connected again when the medicine is finished.*
*The PICC line must be flushed so fluids will
flow easily. If the line becomes clogged, it may have
to be removed.* (Cystic Fibrosis Foundation 2006)

The nurses came to my room to place the line in my arm. The room had to be very sterile to prevent any bacteria from infecting the line. So they had all these blue sheets all over me and the room. The nurses were dressed in sterile clothing as well. Once they were finished, my arm was a little sore, but nothing I couldn't handle. So now I had three intravenous access lines coming out my right arm so I can receive my treatments administered at the same times.

About thirty minutes later, my sister Marcia and nephew Josh came in along with my mom, dad, and my husband still being there. A woman from the research department came in and wanted me to sign all these papers allowing the research team to test me as part of a study on African American women and leukemia. I signed about twenty-five sheets of paper and had a stack to read. Which I had no interest in reading at that time! I had just been having a devastating day, and reading was not what I was ready to do. One good thing about the day was that the initial diagnosis was wrong, and I had a cancer that was curable in three years. Amen!

It seemed like I had a lot of family around my room, calling me on the phone, just overwhelming attention that I was not used to. I had not been able to sleep the whole day, just thinking about what I had to do to make sure my family didn't have to worry too much. So they immediately started my series of treatment which included blood, plasma, and platelet transfusions. I received this almost every hour on the hour, in the midst of them checking my blood count three times a day for about fifteen days straight. This treatment was to increase my red and white blood cells count.

My family was not leaving me in the hospital alone, and I did not want to be left alone so my mom, Sharon, and Marcia took turns staying with me. I remember during the first week, Marcia stayed with me, and the heater had gone out in the house, and he had called me to ask me what he was to do. I don't know how I knew what to do, but I told him to take my children over to Marilyn's and call the number on the furnace. He had it fixed promptly, though. I don't know why he called me instead of figuring it out himself. I think he just wanted me to feel like I still could handle business while being sick. Marcia just shook her head and kept reading her book. If that was Sharon, she would have been very upset. Sharon probably would have taken the phone and hung it up (giggling).

After about day 15, I really started forgetting things, so I asked my family to start writing everything down for me so I could remember later. So from around December 20, and onward, they would write everything down in a composition notebook for me. I didn't necessarily know if I was going to read it all one day, or if I just wanted it as a keepsake for future reference. It was my journey diary with questions I had for the doctors, daily checkup numbers, treatments, things the nurses and doctors may have said that I should know about and remember, and visitors in person or calling on the phone. I was surrounded by love!

My hospital stay treatment started on December 11, 2008, and went on until I was released on January 11, 2009. My treatment consisted of receiving blood, platelets, and plasma. This procedure was followed daily to get my red and white blood counts elevated. What they were doing was taking out my old blood and replacing it with new blood to build up my system. Since APL is a blood cancer, they needed my blood to adjust to the three treatment cycles which would build up my immune system. I had received so much blood, platelets, and plasma that the nurses started making jokes that if anyone was in need, to come see Mrs. Tracy-Thompson (*laughing*). However, it seemed like the more blood I received, the more they were taking. I could taste every treatment they gave me through the IV. It was oh-so nasty on the back of my tongue. I survived it! Even when they had to keep cleaning my PICC lines with a flush, I tasted it (yuck). Remember that each time they gave me medicine, the lines must be flushed before the medicine is administered in the IV. So just imagine how often I had this done. Plus they had to change the dressing around it weekly to prevent infection. I could not even take a shower for weeks because of this line, I could only be washed up. I did not like that at all! That was the main reason I did not enlist in the military (smile)!

Since my mouth was so parched, Birney gave me these lemon-flavored drops that I could put on the back of my tongue to dissolve until I could at least drink. I guess they served the purpose, but I was still thirsty. I remember because I could taste everything that came through my PICC lines that I did not want to eat, just drink. My family made me eat, though! Just the two flavors together would turn my stomach (yuck). If Sharon was there, she would threaten me with Ensure if I didn't eat. One day, I really couldn't eat, so she made me drink the strawberry Ensure (face frowning); it was disgusting to say the least. I was mad at her that day, but I know she was only trying to make sure I stayed strong. Sharon was the thorn on my side, I must say, this whole time (smiling)! I greatly appreciate it now, but during my treatment, I did not.

The one thing my family did not want me to do was to stop eating. They knew if I did not eat, I had nothing to fight with. However, they did not need to worry too much because I wanted to get home to see my children and watch them grow. I had my own mission; I just needed for them to make sure I stayed on course (thumbs up). I knew if I could get past this hospital stay, I was going to be fine. I push myself more than others can challenge me (smiling).

So every morning (around 6:00 a.m. or 7:00 a.m.), the resident doctor on staff would come and ask me how I felt, if I had any questions for the doctor, what happened overnight, and tell me the team of doctors would be in later. They would sometimes tell me what was going to take place that day, if it had to be taken care of before the doctor came in. The team of doctors, at first, would come between 9:30 a.m. and 11:30 a.m., but the further along I got, they started coming later like around noon or 2:00 p.m. I was doing so well that the nurses stopped checking on me as much as well. They would only come in to give me my meds or check my blood. When Sharon was there, she would do everything for me, so they really did not come in but to do the medication and blood. She was doing the nurses' jobs and the nurse techs' job. From helping me take a shower to sanitizing the room and sanitizing and fixing my bed, she was making sure I was germ-free (laughing).

I remember they had this shower cap that could wash your hair without using water; all you had to do was warm it in the microwave for about thirty minutes, and you could put it on your hair to massage your scalp. I loved this cap! Since I couldn't really wash my hair, this was even better than going to the beauty salon and having your hair shampooed. I was in heaven when they gave me this. I wanted it every day! Sharon would get down massaging my head, though, and it was hot (oh my goodness, what a blessing)!

Since the team of doctors was coming so late, I would be in agony, waiting for the test results, to inquire if I could go home or not. My red and white blood count had to be at a certain count before I could be released from the hospital. So for about fifteen to twenty days, I asked everyday if I could go home, and the doctor would kindly say, "Not today." However, I knew when they would come later that the chances of my counts being high enough for me to go home was not going to be on that late day. So I would just wait and ask every day until that day they say I could go home to my babies (persistent).

By December 23, my main doctor was Dr. Maria Baer, professor of medicine in cancers such as hematology/oncology and hematologic malignancies with special interest in acute leukemia and myelodysplastic syndrome (abnormal blood counts). She was going to be the doctor I would see in the UM Marlene and Stewart Greenebaum Cancer Center as an outpatient once I was released for further treatment. Dr. Baer is very knowledgeable when it comes to treating leukemia. Since I was a rare study for them, they just treated me as they would a Latino, since it's more of a Latino cancer. It was fine with me as long as I got cured!

I did have some complications along the way while in the hospital. I found out I was allergic to morphine and a slight heart murmur. With some medicines, I had to get antibiotics because they did not react as they thought. I developed thrush on the back of my tongue which hurt. I would scrape it with my fingernail, it was so thick on my tongue. I can see why babies just cry. I kept saying, "How did

I get thrush, that's for children?" All the different treatments and medicines caused the reaction. I also kept a sore throat and congested nose because the ventilation in the room was so dry. They tried treating it with a nasal spray, but it just had to run its course, I guess.

I spent Christmas 2008, in the hospital. My parents; sisters Joan and Marilyn; brother-in-laws Vernon and Calvin; niece and goddaughter, Tara; and Ms. Anna (deceased), Calvin's mom, came to eat Christmas dinner with me provided by the hospital. While we were eating, Calvin kept saying he didn't feel well and passed out. The nurse's station had called code blue on Calvin, but he was awake, which was a blessing. I was sent back to my room while my sisters were acting all scared (but they are scaredy-cats anyway!). They had sent Calvin to the ER for testing, and he was admitted for two days, diagnosed with high blood pressure. So he was on the other side of the hospital while I was on the transfusion side. What a coincidence! Good thing I was there because he could have been somewhere else, not getting immediate care which could have turned out differently. So we are blessed! He said when he came to, all he could remember was his sister sitting across from him, looking like Grace Jones (laughing). He was talking about me and my hair sticking straight up on my head because it wouldn't lay down plus it was a short cut. As long as he was okay, I could be the butt of the joke (smile).

Later that day, Kelvin came with my children and stepchildren for a little while (they had to make their Christmas rounds with his side of the family). My children were so young they were not allowed to visit me in my room. I had to go out into the lobby area with a mask over my nose and mouth, pulling my medicine monitor. Everyone gave me hugs and kisses but Layden. My son would not come to me, at all, which broke my heart because he was mommy's baby. Fortunately my baby girl, Kayla, told me all about what she and Layden had gotten from Santa Claus and other family (she always spoke for her brother). She had been talking for so long and being a little lady that it was natural for her to ask questions and answer for herself and her little brother. She is my 411 baby and so smart and cute!

I brought in New Year's 2009 with my mom and nurse Birney. While Kelvin and the children came later. My children, being so young, the visits were so short which I hated, but I did it. New Year's 2009, all I wanted was to be cured from cancer and for God to show me the way. What a year!

During my last five days, I was also diagnosed with MRSA. You have probably heard of MRSA but really have never understood how it affects a person's health. So what is MRSA or Methicillin-resistant Staphylococcus aureus?

It is a bacterium that causes infections in different parts of the body. It's tougher to treat than most strains of staphylococcus aureus—or staph—because it's resistant to some commonly used antibiotics. The symptoms of MRSA depend on where you're infected. Most often, it causes mild infections on the skin, like sores or boils. But it can also cause more serious skin infections or infect surgical wounds, the bloodstream, the lungs, or the urinary tract.

Though most MRSA infections aren't serious, some can be life-threatening. Many public health experts are alarmed by the spread of tough strains of MRSA. Because it's hard to treat, MRSA is sometimes called a "super bug."

It is caused by garden-variety staph which are common bacteria that can live in our bodies. Plenty of healthy people carry staph without being infected by it. In fact, one third of everybody has staph bacteria in their noses.

But staph can be a problem if it manages to get into the body, often through a cut. Once there, it can cause an infection. Staph is one of the most common causes of skin infections in the U.S. Usually, these are minor and don't need special treatment. Less often, staph can cause serious problems like infected wounds or pneumonia.

Staph can usually be treated with antibiotics. But over the decades, some strains of staph—like MRSA—have become resistant to antibiotics that once destroyed it. MRSA was first discovered in 1961. It's now resistant to methicillin, amoxicillin, penicillin, oxacillin, and many other common antibiotics.

While some antibiotics still work, MRSA is constantly adapting. Researchers developing new antibiotics are having a tough time keeping up.

So, who can get MRSA? MRSA is spread by contact. So, you could get MRSA by touching another person who has it on the skin. Or you could get it by touching objects that have the bacteria on them. MRSA is carried by about 2% of the population (or 2 in 100 people), although most of them aren't infected.

MRSA infections are common among people who have weak immune systems and are in hospitals, nursing homes, and other health care centers. (WebMD 2015)

Wow, who knew you could contract a virus from being in the hospital so long? This was very interesting to me! There was so much I was learning, and I just kept receiving the knowledge because the more I knew, the better off I would be to help myself and others once I got well. I love to learn!

So now because of my lengthy hospital stay, I have a *green* sign on my door, and everyone who came in the room or was staying with me must wear a gown, gloves, and a face mask for protection from me. Now this was embarrassing to me because it was nothing I did but because I was in the hospital for such a long time, I have the green (you have germs) sign posted on my door. Yes, I was ready to go then for real! Unfortunately before I could leave the hospital, I had to gain my strength back from being in the bed so long. So every day, for about ten to twenty days, I would walk the blood transfusion hallway. It wasn't a long hallway but just enough to get my bones, lungs, and muscles moving. At first, it was a chore to just walk fifteen steps. Fortunately it kept getting easier the more I would walk. So I would walk back and forth in the hallway at least three times a day with my mom, Marcia, or Sharon, whoever was there to stay with me that week. Upon them telling me I could go home, I was a walking sensation (laughing).

A few days before my release, I noticed that my hair was coming out on my pillows and bed. The daunorubicin had me losing my hair in patches, so I let it go. My hair was already cut in a short style, so I figured I would shave it off, instead of every time I lift my head, I had a ball of hair looking at me. I had asked him to bring the clippers so he could shave my head, but he declined (what a chicken). So on January 8, 2009, I had Sharon shave my head bald. Wow, was I surprised at the result (smiling). I had a pretty nice-shaped head! I immediately thought, *Now I have nothing to worry about as far as my looks are concerned.* Yeah, a little ego trip! The only concern was that it was in the middle of the winter, and I decided to go completely bald. What timing I have!

During this time, I also received instructions on how to care for my PICC line, what I was and was not allowed to eat, staying germ-free, a list of prescriptions I needed, and all the things I accumulated from staying for thirty-one days. The doctor came in and told me what my next steps would be of treatment but as an outpatient in the cancer center. They told me I had to go back to the cancer clinic in a week for further treatment. My treatment would consist of five weeks of chemo, five days a week, then off for two weeks, and go back for the next set of five weeks of chemo, five days a week. I would be on ATRA pills for one and a half years. This treatment plan would have me cured in three years, totally cured in five. I was ecstatic!

On January 11, 2009, at 10:00 a.m., I was told I could go home, but I did not get all my discharge papers until 5:00 p.m. or 6:00 p.m. It took so long I ate lunch and dinner before going home. They did end up moving me to the cancer side that day where I ate dinner. The room they were trying to put me in smelled like someone had just passed away in it. The nurse tech had cleaned and sanitized it, but the smell was still there. I would not go into that room until they got that smell out. She ended up taking all the bedding, even the pillows in the closet, out trying to get rid of the smell. All this time, I was sitting on a wheelchair in the hallway, refusing to enter. Sharon got so irritated she started cleaning the room herself. Finally they got rid of the smell after about thirty minutes, and I could go into the room. Since the diagnosis, my senses were so high, I could hear, smell, see, and taste everything (good and bad). I remember having spaghetti for dinner, and I did not want to eat it because my stomach was upset. So here Sharon goes, threatening me with this stupid Ensure tactic! I tried to eat it, but it would not stay down. She was getting irritated now because I was really feeling sick to the stomach, and it all came back up (yuck). It was weird because the spaghetti came back up just like it looked on the plate, as if my body did not digest it. It was the craziest thing I had ever seen! I did eat the fruit and pudding. So after I ate, we received the discharge papers, and Kelvin and the children came to pick Sharon and me up.

When I got in the truck, the children were looking at me crazy because I was bald. Then when I got home, I was so overwhelmed. My children were running around, everything just seemed to be going so fast, and I felt like going back to the hospital. All I could do was sit on the sofa and stare! Sharon hugged me and said, "It's too much, huh?" I just nodded my head yes! Then she said, "But you were so ready to come home, and I told you that it was going to be too much." I was mad at her for that, but I understood. When you hear the truth, sometimes it is a hard pill to swallow, but it needed to be said and you needed to hear it. However, I knew I had the resilience to keep surviving.

RESILIENCE TO KEEP SURVIVING

*What lies behind you and what lies in front of you
pales in comparison to what lies inside of you.*

—Ralph Waldo Emerson

CANCER

When you hear you have cancer, the thoughts that go through your mind are endless: How did this happen? Did I do something wrong? Am I being punished? Is God trying to tell me something? Then comes the blame, denial, grief, fear, and acceptance. Now is it terminal? Can it be cured? Is it hereditary? Or am I being used as a vessel. Well, all these thoughts are true. However, what happens when you are diagnosed with a cancer that is not hereditary, not for your age, ethnicity, culture, sex, or socioeconomic class? Somehow it is curable in three years, according to research, and even totally cured in five years. It is not even thought of or heard of, right? So we think!

Now you are a person who hardly ever got sick; you took care of your body, you paid attention to your body's symptoms, and made sure you maintained as little stress as possible. Unfortunately you are not exempt when it comes to cancer. Cancer does not have your name on it, but we all have cancerous cells in our bodies. I believe God knows how to grab your attention when he needs to step in your life before you sink or swim. This would have to do with where you stand in your faith as to if you believe or not that God is in control of your destiny. He is in control of mine!

Well, this is me! After six years of being cancer-free, I felt it is time to tell my life's journey so that I may be of help to at least one person, if not many, who have gone through cancer or who is going through it now (it is now eleven and a half years). In addition, I was being encouraged and pestered by so many to tell my story because I am a walking miracle (smiling) that I thought, now is the time. I can honestly say that positive thinking and support are key factors in helping you go through the battle as well as putting your faith in a higher power that He is working with the doctors, whom I believe He has preselected to care for you. Just hearing the word *cancer* is scary enough, so you need everything that your faith has to work in your favor.

On October 25, 2008, I caught what I thought was the flu because it had me down and out for more than fifteen days. However, I didn't have any health insurance, so I was basically trying to let it take its course. But it never really got better, and I needed to go back to work because I was now self-employed which meant I needed some income to take care of my family. So I tried willing myself back from whatever was trying to take over my body. On Monday, December 2, 2008, my parents came down to help me install my new stove. While they were here, I was trying to put up drywall to cut off an entrance area to the kitchen from my children's bedroom. Usually I could have done this without any problem. but this day, I was having problems. My arms were shaking when I was trying to drill, I could barely pick up the drywall, and my focus was off. So my dad had to complete it because I just couldn't do it by myself. This was a sign! I had my first CDA training class under my consulting business on Friday, December 5, 2008, at Sunshine Early Learning Center for the Southeast Children's Fund PDI-P3 program. I did not feel my best, so I had him take me to work just in case. Shortly after I got there, I became very ill. I did teach class, but my body was going through all kinds of changes that I couldn't understand. So I had to have him come pick me up from work because I was that sick. I remember lying in the back seat of our Yukon Denali XL with Layden sitting in his car seat on the second row and not wanting to get up. I felt like crap!

When I got home, I was so sick with migraine, diarrhea, chills, shortness of breath, fatigue, vomiting, nausea, dehydration, and body aches, especially in my bones the entire weekend. I had been complaining that my bones were aching throughout the year, but I thought it was due to the weight gain I had from Layden. Even though I had been breastfeeding, I was not losing any weight. I just thought it was me getting older which made it hard for me to lose the weight fast. Never once did I think it was something life threatening.

I was becoming dehydrated and lethargic at times. I searched for the coolest place in the house because I could not get comfortable. At the time, he was complaining that he was a little ill too, but not like me, so he took care of the children while I was trying to recover. However, I was so sick that Kayla and Layden tried to help me get better by holding me and bringing me something to eat and drink (they knew something was wrong with their mommy). But on Monday, December 8, 2008, at 6:25 a.m., I began bleeding from my rectum, filling up the entire toilet. I did not suffer from hemorrhoids or anything else for that matter. Right then, I knew something serious was wrong, and I couldn't fight this on my own. I was seriously dehydrated that my tongue and mouth were white; my rationale started to fade, and my strength was completely gone. Even though I was drinking liters and liters of water and ginger ale. I thought to myself, *I have no health insurance so what am I going to do*! I had called Kelvin to tell him what was going on, and he called his mother, Roxanne. Ms. Roxanne said that she would call her doctor, Dr. Fahad Jamali, and see what he could do. They both knew this was a serious situation, and I needed medical attention. Dr. Fahad Jamali advised her to take me to Prince George's Hospital's emergency room in Landover, Maryland, and he would call so I could go straight to a room instead of sitting in the ER, waiting. So I managed to get Layden (who was only fourteen months) and myself dressed so that I could go to the hospital, and Layden could go over to Marilyn's house who lived just around the corner from us. He was head coach for McNamara's high school freshman basketball team, and they had a game that night; so I told him to go ahead because I would be all right. I was so out of it, though. I remember dropping Layden off, and I couldn't even take him in (worried). I gave him a kiss and told him Mommy would be back later. Unbeknownst to me, that would be thirty-three days later.

Heart Failure

However, on December 5, 2009, while shopping for the children's Christmas things, I noticed I was short of breath when I was walking a short distance. My stomach had gotten so big it looked as if I was nine months pregnant. I thought it had something to do with the tubal ligation, so I went to the gynecologist to see if something was wrong. No, it was not from that! I could not figure out what was wrong with me. I thought it was from the Turkey Hill lemonade I was drinking (smiling). Just trying to eliminate things before I went to the ER (self-diagnosing). Since he was planning to go with the basketball team to Las Vegas for Christmas, he asked me if anything was wrong before he planned to go on this trip. I told him about what was happening to me and that I wanted to go to the ER to have some test run, just to make sure nothing major was causing my stomach to expand, and he could go on his trip, not worrying about me. I thought he really cared about me, but how I was so wrong!

On December 16, 2009, I asked him to take me to the emergency room because I was not feeling good at all, and my stomach was getting bigger while my breathing was getting shorter. I had taken the children over to Marilyn's already so we could just go without having to drop them off first. He began arguing with me, and he did this for a few hours before taking me to the ER. He was walking around the house, saying all types of mean hurtful things because now I was messing with his trip if I was admitted to the hospital. He had been drinking and commented that's all he has time to do since I was always sick. I could not believe what was happening. I just knew I needed to get to the hospital. The more I argued with him and the more upset I was getting, the less breaths I was getting. He had me crying, so you know what I was thinking about doing once I got well—divorce. I wasn't ever going to let a man make me cry when it had to do with my health or taking care of my needs. I would or will do anything for the one I supposedly love, so I made up my mind, *You sit here and argue with me over some bull crap trip you might not be able to go on because I keep getting sick! Our relationship in my eyes is done!* I meant that! I was sick and fighting every day for my life, and he was so selfish he couldn't see anything but what he needed for him. That was just it for me, selfish will be selfless without me and my children!

Once I got in the emergency room and they ran some tests, the doctor told me not to get out of bed anymore. I was going to the bathroom a lot, so I needed to walk there because I could not hold it. She told me, in a very stern voice, not to get back out of bed for any reason. This whole time, he was in the room, on the chair, asleep, smelling like a brewery. I just let him be! Then the doctor told me that the cardiologist would be in to see me. I couldn't figure out what the heart doctor had to do with my stomach and breathing. Came to find out, I had congestive heart failure (water around my heart). They told me that it was probably from the daunorubicin I received earlier. This will be explained later in the chapter "Cure for Tomorrow's Health" under "Important Warning."

I could not believe it, another obstacle (shaking my head). They informed me that my heart was only beating at 10 percent and that I had a 30 percent chance of it getting worse, 30 percent chance of it staying the same, and a 30 percent chance it would improve. At that moment, I prayed and told the Lord once I am out of this clear, I am getting divorced because something in my life is not healthy for me, and after the stunt he pulled, I did not want to be bothered with him anymore. My parents came and stayed with me for a few weeks. He did not leave to go to Las Vegas, though, so I don't know if he just felt he shouldn't go, or he knew that my family would have consequences for him when he came back. I am not saying he was afraid of my family, but my family does not play when it comes to me.

I was put on some blood pressure pills, Lasix for water, and heart rate medicine (three more medications). To me, this was a lot, but I wanted to stay around for my babies, so I took it with a grain of salt. I couldn't help but to say, "Lord, obstacle after obstacle, what is it that you want me to see or do that I am not doing?" I could not put my finger on it! Fortunately I was aware of my own courage, so I pushed to the next obstacle.

AWARENESS OF MY OWN COURAGE

You were given this life because you are strong enough to live it.

—Unknown

Since I was so aware of my own courage, I kept a positive attitude and knew God was on my side. Unfortunately on Wednesday, December 10, at Prince George's Community Hospital, around 10:00 a.m., the doctor, fellows, residents, interns, and a priest came into my room to give me the results of all the test they had taken (there were about nine individuals in white coats, standing around my hospital bed, and a priest with a stack full of books). I was using the bathroom, still bleeding from my rectum, when they entered. So imagine walking out the bathroom, looking at all these doctors standing around your bed. The head doctor was sitting on the heater, Indian style (like he was about to meditate or something, smiling). The fellows and residents had their arms crossed in a stern position. Then this priest, with about ten to fifteen books in his hand, was about to read me my last will and testament (eyes wide open). What would you be thinking at this moment (seriously?).

I could not really concentrate on what the doctor was telling me because of the priest with those books (very observant). The doctor asked me if anyone in my family had leukemia at first, I said my sister because I thought he said lupus. Then I realized what he said, and I replied my half-niece when she was a child, but I didn't know what type. I do know she needed a bone marrow transplant from her little sister to survive. So I asked, "Why are you asking me that?"

He replied, "Because you either have AML or a serious vitamin B12 deficiency."

In a sarcastic tone, I said, "I'll take the serious vitamin B12 deficiency, doctor (smiling)!"

He said in a very nice soft voice, "I don't think that's your choice, I strongly believe it's leukemia."

Being sarcastic again—"Why did you give me a choice then if you knew what it was?" (smirk). Now I feel like he tricked me (ugh)!

So I asked him, "What does this mean, and shouldn't I have been told this news with a family member present?" He ignored my comment about the family member and proceeded to tell me that I would have to be transferred to the University of Maryland Medical Center or Johns Hopkins in Baltimore, Maryland, for further testing because they did not have the capability or was equipped to handle leukemia patients. He said more than likely the University of Maryland Medical Center, though. I said, "As long as it is somewhere my family can get to easily."

Then he went on to ask me if I was okay, I replied yes. Thinking to myself, *How the heck do you think I feel? You just told me I have cancer* (sarcastic look). So I just asked what it was that I needed to do and what is the likelihood this was terminal. He told me to keep the faith and stay positive, but if it is AML, I would only have two years to live, max. That struck a nerve (I fell back on the bed)! Thinking, *I don't believe God would take me away from my babies like this. He does have a sense of humor but not like this (shaking my head in denial). And I still have a lot to live for, and I intend on doing just that.* My thoughts immediately started working because I had a lot to consider in a very short period.

Everyone left out the room. Then the priest, with his stack of books, came back in after about a minute and asked me if I needed anything and proceeded to give me books to read, but I declined. I replied, "I will be fine. God is in control now!" He asked me if I wanted to pray, but I declined because I needed this time to talk to my God on my own! I needed my faith in the Holy Spirit to take over my body now so that I could be healed. So I lay back on the bed for a minute or so to take it all in and to figure out what and how I was going to tell my family I had acute myeloid leukemia. I knew they were going to have a lot of questions that I could not answer and that they were going to be very distraught with this news. I knew I had to pick my words wisely because I did not want to set them off. I need them to be strong for me like I am strong for them. I had to keep things under control until I could figure out what God had planned (optimistic).

According to Wikipedia (February 2015):

> **Acute myeloid leukemia (AML)**, *also known as* **acute myelogenous leukemia** *or* **acute non-lymphocytic leukemia (ANLL)**, *is a cancer of the myeloid line of blood cells, characterized by the rapid growth of abnormal white blood cells that accumulate in the bone marrow and interfere with the production of normal blood cells. AML is the most common acute leukemia affecting adults, and its incidence increases with age. Although AML is a relatively rare disease, accounting for approximately 1.2% of cancer deaths in the United States, its incidence is expected to increase as the population ages.*
>
> *The symptoms of AML are caused by replacement of normal bone marrow with leukemic cells, which causes a drop in red blood cells, platelets, and normal white blood cells. These symptoms include fatigue, shortness of breath, easy bruising and bleeding, and increased risk of infection. Several risk factors and chromosomal abnormalities have been identified, but the specific cause is not clear. As an acute leukemia, AML progresses rapidly and is typically fatal within weeks or months if left untreated.*
>
> *AML has several subtypes; treatment and prognosis varies among subtypes. Five-year survival varies from 15–70%, and relapse rate varies from 33–78%, depending on subtype. AML is treated initially with chemotherapy aimed at inducing a remission; patients may go on to receive additional chemotherapy or a hematopoietic stem cell transplant. Recent research into the genetics of AML has resulted in the availability of tests that can predict*

which drug or drugs may work best for a particular patient, as well as how long that patient is likely to survive.

I was transferred to the University of Maryland Bone Marrow Transplant Unit at the medical center. I arrived at approximately midnight, December 11, 2008, and greeted by nurse Birney and tech Jackie. They advised me that a lot of test were going to be ran and much poking would take place later, so I needed to try and get some rest. I thought to myself, Okay, but I'm not going to sleep.

Later that day, many tests took place and much family started to visit. At about 5:00 p.m., the team of doctors came with the results of all the test. By this time, I think there were about ten family members in my room (love). They told me that if I could have picked any type of cancer, I have the best one because it's curable in three years. I was diagnosed with acute promyelocytic leukemia which has been studied in Japan and has a curable rate of three years and totally curable in five years. It was very rare in African Americans, especially females in their thirties, but it is APL!

According to Genetic Home Reference (March 2015):

Acute promyelocytic leukemia is a form of acute myeloid leukemia, a cancer of the blood-forming tissue (bone marrow). In normal bone marrow, hematopoietic stem cells produce red blood cells (erythrocytes) that carry oxygen, white blood cells (leukocytes) that protect the body from infection, and platelets (thrombocytes) that are involved in blood clotting. In acute promyelocytic leukemia, immature white blood cells called promyelocytes accumulate in the bone marrow. The overgrowth of promyelocytes leads to a shortage of normal white and red blood cells and platelets in the body, which causes many of the signs and symptoms of the condition.

Acute promyelocytic leukemia individuals are especially susceptible to developing bruises, small red dots under the skin (petechiae), nosebleeds, bleeding from the gums, blood in the urine (hematuria), or excessive menstrual bleeding. The abnormal bleeding and bruising occur in part because of the low number of platelets in the blood (thrombocytopenia) and also because the cancerous cells release substances that cause excessive bleeding.

The low number of red blood cells (anemia) can cause individuals with acute promyelocytic leukemia to have pale skin (pallor) or excessive tiredness (fatigue). In addition, affected individuals may heal slowly from injuries or have frequent infections due to the loss of normal white blood cells that fight infection. Furthermore, the leukemic cells can spread to the bones and joints, which may cause pain in those areas. Other general signs and symptoms may occur as well, such as fever, loss of appetite, and weight loss.

Acute promyelocytic leukemia is most often diagnosed around age 40, although it can be diagnosed at any age. However, acute promyelocytic leukemia accounts for about 10 percent of acute myeloid leukemia cases. Acute promyelocytic leukemia occurs in approximately 1 in 250,000 people in the United States.

The mutation that causes acute promyelocytic leukemia involves two genes, the PML gene on chromosome 15 and the RARA gene on chromosome 17. A rearrangement of genetic material (translocation) between chromosomes 15 and 17, written as t (15; 17), fuses part of the PML gene with part of the RARA gene. The protein produced from this fused gene is known as PML-RARa. This mutation is acquired during a person's lifetime and is present only in certain cells. This type of genetic change, called a somatic mutation, is not inherited.

*The PML-RARa protein functions differently
than the protein products of the normal PML and
RARAgenes. The protein produced from the RARA
gene, RARa, is involved in the regulation of gene
transcription, which is the first step in protein pro-
duction. Specifically, this protein helps control the
transcription of certain genes important in the mat-
uration (differentiation) of white blood cells beyond
the promyelocyte stage. The protein produced from
the PML gene acts as a tumor suppressor, which
means it prevents cells from growing and dividing
too rapidly or in an uncontrolled way. The PML-
RARa protein interferes with the normal function of
both the PML and the RARa proteins. As a result,
blood cells are stuck at the promyelocyte stage, and
they proliferate abnormally. Excess promyelocytes
accumulate in the bone marrow and normal white
blood cells cannot form, leading to acute promyelocytic leukemia.*

*The PML-RARA gene fusion accounts for up
to 98 percent of cases of acute promyelocytic leukemia. Translocations involving the RARA gene and
other genes have been identified in a few cases of
acute promyelocytic leukemia.*

*Acute promyelocytic leukemia is not inherited
but arises from a translocation in the body's cells that
occurs after conception.*

All I could think about was how good my God is and thank
you, Jesus! I was nowhere close to being out of the clear, but this
wasn't a cancer I would die from which was the ultimate blessing for
me. I am a fighter, so I was going to be totally cured in five years,
guaranteed.

My family had asked if they needed to give blood, just in case
I needed a bone marrow match, but the doctor said since all my siblings were my half-siblings that by them donating, it would be like

a stranger's donation. The only matches that would be most considered was my father or my children. I wasn't thinking that far ahead and figured we would tackle it when we came across the situation. I did not believe I would need a bone marrow, so I wasn't worried!

Then the studies lady came in the room to tell me that she heard the good news and to tear up all those papers she had me sign earlier that day. I was not going to be needing them because I had a better cancer outcome. Next the social worker came in and signed me up for health insurance because I did not have any at the time. She had me fill out everything right then and had me signed up for health care in three days. That was a relief! She also gave me papers to fill out with my power of attorney for my medical and a temporary will. I just sat it to the side for a day or two.

I decided not to put him in charge of my medical needs because he wasn't acting like he would make the best decision for me. He was not there enough for me, and I worried about if he would make the decision like I would want him to. So I made my niece my power of attorney because she thought like me and would confide in family before making any decisions. I was very confident about it! This was when I knew I had courage in myself to pull through whatever I had to. God had a plan for me, and if I stayed the course, He was going to see me through with awareness, hope, trust, and strength. Just thinking about the cure for tomorrow's health brings awareness to the courage that I possessed.

CURE FOR TOMORROW'S HEALTH

The difference between the impossible and the possible lies in a person's determination.

—Tommy Lasorda

After a day or two, all I remember was telling my family that I did not want to be left alone because it felt like I was starting to lose my memory. I was informed that I would have to stay in the hospital until my counts went up which could take anywhere between fifteen and thirty days. I was flabbergasted because that meant I would be spending Christmas and New Year's in the hospital, away from my children (tears). This was really going to be hard to be away from my babies for the holiday. But I had to do it because I would never miss another holiday away from my children and family again.

Over the next three days, they checked me for everything. They needed to make sure my body was able to function properly with all the treatment I was to endure and for a speedy recovery. I went to the dentist, a gynecologist came in, and my eyes were checked, especially since I have glaucoma, an ultrasound of my heart and stomach, X-rays, CAT scans, MRI, and every possible thing you can have checked was checked. I may have left out something, but they left out nothing! I remember having a migraine so bad that they took me out of my room in my bed to the neurologist's exam room. I had to wait because others were ahead of me (I fell asleep waiting). Once the nurse rolled me back to my floor, he left me in the hallway, I guess thinking the nurses could roll me in my room. I had the sheet over my head, so everyone just kept walking by me. I assume they did not think anyone was in the bed. Finally someone bumped into the bed, and I pulled the covers off my head and saw my mom and Marcia sitting in my room talking. So once I pulled the covers back, the nurse rolled me back into the room. I had been in the hallway for about two hours before I was bumped. When I got back into the room, my mom and Marcia said they saw the bed sitting there but didn't know it was me. I couldn't even get upset because my head was pounding with pain.

Because they could do most test in the room, there was little concern of that happening again. Everything came back negative, so nothing was going to stop my treatment plan. The neurologist's test came back negative for anything being wrong with the nerves in my brain to be causing me to have such terrible migraines. However, I kept the migraine for about seven days before the pain started to subside. They never knew why I had the migraine, but I was glad it went away. I think the blood transfusions were making me better. Every now and then, I would get one but not as bad as the initial ones.

My mom and sisters Sharon and Marcia all took turns staying with me. It was a long thirty-one days stay in the hospital, but these three wonderful women in my life made sure they took care of me, and when they slacked sometimes, they let them know it (especially Sharon, she was not playing with my care). I was surrounded by love!

The social worker came back after about three days and asked for the power of attorney papers and will. My family had discussed it with me and told me to make it someone who thought like me and would do what I would do; it couldn't be my mom. So I choose my niece Shayna, who is Sharon's daughter, but she thinks the most like me, just more in touch with her feelings than I would be. I knew, though, she would not do anything without consulting the family first. I did not choose him because I didn't think he would have my best interest at heart, and the nursing staff recommended for me not to put him down (he never knew that). I did not know why they said that, but after the blood transfusion incident, he wasn't going down anyway (nervous). I had to put someone I knew would handle my business correctly. In addition, my family wouldn't let me put him down anyway because they didn't trust his judgment (smiling). They seriously don't play when it comes to family, especially me because I'm the baby!

Sharon spent the first two weeks with me. She was like a drill sergeant the entire time I was sick. There were several incidents that made her skin crawl, but the main one was a night when the nurse, Ms. Jackie, who was about sixty-five to seventy years of age and wore large glasses with thick lenses, short brown hair, heavyset, and short. Just imagine for a second! When she would come in the room to give me meds or to take blood, she would turn on every light in the room (laughing). Sharon would be so disturbed because she not only could not see, but she was slow (laughing). She would get so frustrated she just put the covers over her head with a huge sigh (giggling). I would be laughing at Sharon but also watching because Ms. Jackie would always forget to do something or leave things on my bed. After she would leave the room, Sharon would say, "Damn, she has to turn on every light and be so slow" (giggling). I got used to it, but she never did!

I think the first two weeks were my worst because my senses where very sensitive. I couldn't stand the smell of food, hand sanitizer that was in the room, perfumes/cologne, or the wipes they use to wipe down my bed when they changed my sheets. Since I had migraines, I didn't like loud noises (which weren't necessarily loud) because it triggered my ears to ring and my head to feel like someone was squeezing my head together (ouch). I had to keep the cover over my head because the light would bother me as well. Some days I could cope, but most of those first days, it was hard.

When I had about ten days left in the hospital (yes, I asked to go home for twenty days, *chuckle*), they started giving me my chemo which was ATRA (pills) and daunorubicin (IV). I only had the daunorubicin for about three to five days. In addition, the ATRA was what I had to go home with and take for the next one and a half years, so I needed to know what I was taking. What is ATRA and daunorubicin going to do?

ATRA has three different names: *Tretinoin, Vesanoid*·, and *All-trans retinoic acid. ATRA is an anti-cancer ("antineoplastic" or "cytotoxic") chemotherapy drug. ATRA is classified as a "retinoid."*

ATRA is used to treat acute promyelocytic leukemia (APL, APML). ATRA works as Retinoids which are drugs that are relatives of vitamin A. Retinoids control normal cell growth, cell differentiation (the normal process of making cells different from each other), and cell death during embryonic development and in certain tissues later in life. Retinoids effects on the cells are controlled by receptors on the nucleus of each cell (nuclear receptors).

There are two major classes of retinoid nuclear receptors: retinoic acid receptors (RAR) and retinoid-X-receptors (RXR). There are also subtypes within each class. Each of these types of receptors has different functions in different tissues. The different retinoid drugs work by binding to different receptors; which, in turn, affect cell growth and differentiation.

Retinoids are relatively new types of anti-cancer drugs. They have been used alone or in combination to treat a variety of cancers such as skin cancers, cutaneous T-cell lymphoma, acute promyelocytic leukemia, lung cancer, breast cancer, ovarian cancer, bladder cancer, kidney cancer, and head and neck cancers. Retinoids have also been used experimentally in an attempt to prevent certain types of cancer. There is ongoing research to determine their role in both cancer treatment and prevention. (chemocare.com, 2015)

According to MedLine Plus (2015):

Daunorubicin is used with other chemotherapy drugs to treat a certain type of acute myeloid leukemia (AML; a type of cancer of the white blood cells). Daunorubicin is also used with other chemotherapy drugs to treat a certain type of acute lymphocytic leukemia (ALL; a type of cancer of the white blood cells). Daunorubicin is in a class of medications called anthracyclines. It works by slowing or stopping the growth of cancer cells in your body.

Daunorubicin comes as a solution (liquid) or as a powder to be mixed with liquid to be injected intravenously (into a vein) by a doctor or nurse in a medical facility along with other chemotherapy medications. When daunorubicin is used to treat AML, it is usually injected once a day on certain days of your treatment period. When daunorubicin is used to treat ALL, it is usually injected once a week. The length of treatment depends on the types of drugs you are taking, how well your body responds to them, and the type of cancer you have.

Daunorubicin may cause side effects such as: nausea, vomiting, sores in the mouth and throat, diarrhea, stomach pain, hair loss, and red urine. Some more serious side effects are: redness, pain, swelling, or burning at the site where the injection was given, rash, hives, itching, and difficulty breathing or swallowing.

Daunorubicin may increase the risk that you will develop other cancers. It is important for you to keep a written list of all of the prescription and nonprescription (over-the-counter) medicines you are taking, as well as any products such as vitamins, minerals, or other dietary supplements. You should bring this list with you each time you visit a doctor or if you are admitted to a hospital. It is also important information to carry with you in case of emergencies.

Other names associates with Daunorubicin are Cerubidine, Daunomycin, and Rubidomycin. (www.nim.nih.gov, 2011)

This warning is important to know for a diagnosis later in the "Remission" chapter of this book.

Important Warning: Daunorubicin injection must be given in a hospital or medical facility under the supervision of a doctor who is experienced in giving chemotherapy medications for cancer.

Daunorubicin may cause serious or life-threatening heart problems at any time during your treatment or months to years after your treatment has ended. Your doctor will order tests before and during your treatment to see if your heart is working well enough for you to safely receive daunorubicin. These tests may include an electrocardiogram (ECG; test that records the electrical activity of the heart) and an echocardiogram (test that uses sound waves to measure your heart's ability to pump blood). Your doctor may tell you that you should not receive this medication if the tests show your heart's ability to pump blood has decreased. Tell your doctor if you have or have ever had any type of heart disease or radiation (x-ray) therapy to the chest area. If you experience any of the following symptoms, call your doctor immediately: shortness of breath; difficulty breathing; swelling of the hands, feet, ankles or lower legs; or fast, irregular, or pounding heartbeat.

Daunorubicin can cause a severe decrease in the number of blood cells in your bone marrow. This may cause certain symptoms and may increase the risk that you will develop a serious infection or bleeding. If you experience any of the following symptoms, call your doctor immediately: fever, sore throat, ongoing cough and congestion, or other signs of infection; unusual bleeding or bruising.

The day I was released from the hospital, they gave me the prescription of ATRA to get filled at a pharmacy by my home. What a reality check! We could not find any pharmacy to fill my ATRA prescription. We had called every pharmacy in the area, and everyone had to order it, but I had to take it that night. Now Sharon and Marilyn were running crazy, trying to get someone to fill this prescription that day. Unfortunately Kelvin had to drive me back down to UMMC to get two doses from the nurse's station until my prescription could be filled the next day. We went back to Baltimore, Maryland, at 9:00 p.m. which is about forty-five minutes from where we live. If we would have known it was so hard to find it by my home, we could have filled it while we were waiting on the release papers. What a way to end a long hospital stay!

I was released from UMMC on January 11, 2009. So while I was in the hospital and my family found out I had to be germ-free, they came down and cleaned my house (even Kayla) and put in hardwood, laminated floors in my basement because I couldn't be around mold or mildew. This meant my carpet in the basement had to be pulled up so they could put me in a new floor. They did all this for me! I love my family! I found out that Kelvin didn't help which was not a good look for him at this moment. But I wasn't surprised!

Upon my discharge, I was instructed to go back to the cancer center in a week as an outpatient to receive further care. So I went home and returned on January 14, 2009. While I was giving blood, the nurse told me that I would be getting a bone marrow biopsy that day. I was immediately terrified because the first one I had was horrific to say the least. I do remember asking the doctor when I received the first one if I could be put to sleep the next time, and he agreed. Well, I guess it slipped their mind to put it in my records, so now I was at this crossroad. My mom and dad were there with me when I got the news. My heart was beating so fast and hard I thought you could see it coming out of my shirt (scared). I just remember feeling the pit of my stomach hurting! I was mentally sick!

Nurse practitioner Mike Tidwell (deceased) came in the room to introduce himself and asked me if I was ready. With much confidence, I said, "*No!*" I told him that the doctor agreed that I could be put to sleep for this procedure. He replied by saying that he would numb me so that it wouldn't be so painful, but if it hurt, I could be put to sleep. I did remember the nurses on the transfusion side telling me to ask for Mike Tidwell because he was the best. It didn't matter because I was still very skeptical. So he had me lie on my stomach, putting my hands under my head, and that he would be going through my right hip bone to get the bone marrow. He did a good job because it was nowhere near the pain I had the first time. NP Mike did say that he understood why the fellows had so much trouble and why it hurt me so bad. He said I had the strongest bones he had ever had to perform the procedure on in his career. Now I kind of understood but didn't understand. I had to lie flat on my back for fifteen minutes with this thick gauze pad over the incision to stop the bleeding. Once he saw the bleeding had stopped, I could go home. He gave me medicine for the pain. However, once the medicine wore off, I could not stand, lie down flat, or walk because my side hurt terribly. The puncture wasn't that big nor did it bleed heavily, but I had to keep the bandage on for a few days.

I endured this ghastly pain for about five days or so. I did have pain medicine, but it could not withstand the pain that I was feeling. NP Mike told me that I would have to get these procedures every three months for the next three years. *So again, you are telling me this is going to be my life for the next three years every three months* (yikes). My heart just ached! So now that the pain medication was not really going to take the pain away, I must figure out how I was going to cope with this pain. Unfortunately the pain was so bad I couldn't just cope with it, I needed relief. So now I was silently fighting within my soul, and I must learn how to cope!

SILENT FIGHTER WITHIN ONE'S SOUL

Sometimes the hardest thing and the right thing are the same

—Unknown

L et's go back to the beginning so you can understand why I have ben silently fighting within my soul for a long time, so by the time the cancer came, I have some experience as to how I was going to cope. As I grew up, I rarely ever missed school because of an illness. I did have pneumonia when I was five months old and was hospitalized, but nothing until I became a young adult. I was a pretty healthy and stress-free child (so I thought). I didn't want for anything, and I challenged myself to be the best of the best and not to let anyone or thing get in my way. Even in the tough teenage years, I played basketball, took gymnastics (tap), sang in the school chorus and the NAACP Young Adult Choir, and took school seriously. I had two main friends throughout school (Bridgett and Trini). I have known Trini since kindergarten and Bridgett since second grade. We grew up together, but as adults, we went on separate paths; as you can see, they are a minister, minister of music and reverend, and I am an entrepreneur in education and business. But believe you me, God is at the forefront of everything I did, do, and will do (smiling). I also had a friend from the neighborhood, Lorie, but once she moved, our friendship wasn't as close even though we call each other sisters.

Now I had more individuals I associated with, but I really didn't get into having many friends, or what I referred to as my associates, because I was always skeptical of why they wanted to be around me (critical thinker). I had some ups and downs, but for the most part, nothing more than anyone else. Kids are cruel and they say things to kill your spirit, but I always had faith that could withstand most, so I really didn't care too much what they thought about me. I did have my nieces and nephews to take care of, though (it was rough sometimes, fighting their battles).

My senior year, I started dating a ninth grader, Michael, but we had so much in common, and he was showing me what love really felt like and how it should be reciprocated. I thought we would someday, in the future, make great soul mates. He helped me finish my senior year stress-free because I could talk to him about anything. It was refreshing! Until I met him, I don't think I was open to any of my friends. I told you what I wanted and kept it moving, but with him, it was different which, in turn, was scary. I graduated high school in the third percentile of my class in 1992.

I had so many dreams of my future, I did not want anything to stop or stand in my path of what I thought was my happiness. I was dedicated to so many things that I think I forgot how to live. I met another guy, Omar, who brought a different part out of me. He was away at college, and I could only see him in the summers which was okay since I had my own dreams. He did end up having some obligations during a couple of the summers where he could not see me, but he was older than me, so he graduated with a business degree in economics in 1995. Once he graduated, we hung out a few times, but by this time, we were on two different life paths. We kept in touch for a little while, but once I told him I was moving to Washington, DC, we knew we would only be friends. He did tell me not to fall for any city guy because it was not going to be good, but I did not listen. Interesting, I lost contact with him for seventeen years, but as soon as we talked, he knew something was up with me (giggling). Sometimes I think people giving me advice are giving it for selfish reasons, but this was one I should have adhered to. Well!

I had a difficult time personally in 1995–1996 which ultimately affected my schooling, but I did not quit. I realized that when people are unhappy with their lives or think you have something better than them, they will do anything to kill your spirit and take you out of character. However, I was too keen and strong for all that, so I just kept on pushing through all the unnecessary nonsense. My best friend enlisted in the marines, and my other friend was at school, so I had no one to share these stresses with, but I got through them.

Yes, my sisters were there to help, but they can't fight all my battles, I thought. Funny thing, they sure let me know they had my back as old as they were (giggling).

I met Kelvin in 1997, a few months after I had been violated by someone I knew. I did not tell anyone that this had happened to me, and I made a promise to myself that I would never talk about it again. Unfortunately I must address this because this was a silent fight that I am having within my soul. It was a factor when I first started dating Kelvin because I couldn't trust. I worked it out, but we did have a sketchy five-year relationship before we got married. As they say, "The way he was walking." Which means he was doing things that were not the way I thought a married man should act or a man living with his girlfriend should act. However, once we got married, I played the happy wife for years; but deep down, I became miserable. He did make me laugh, and we got along, but I could never let go of him purchasing that car. Some may think that it was petty of me to disconnect myself with a person because of such a small thing, but when you agree to one thing and you become selfish, I don't have any room for you. I felt he wanted to be a player, and family was not that important to him. We were only important when he wanted to show us off to his friends. LaShawn was surely back (eyes wide open)!

My next encounter with a silent fight within my soul was when I was diagnosed with cancer. I was in such turmoil now that I said a short prayer and shed a tear or two (I'm not a crier, it gives me a headache) for a second, just letting myself exhale before addressing my family. I had made it up in my mind that God gave this to me for a reason, but He is not ready for me yet. I have babies to see grow, and He's not that cruel! I also knew I had to stay strong because if I lost control, my family was going to fall apart because they depended on me. So that's what I did!

I called Kelvin and asked him if he was sitting down, in my regular, calm, nonchalant voice. He said, "Why, what's wrong?" I explained to him what the doctor had said.

He replied, "Get the f—— out of here." I told him yes, it was true. So he asked me how I was and who I wanted him to call first, my mom or Sharon?

I replied with sarcasm, "My mom!" I asked him, why would you call Sharon before my mom (confused)?

He replied, "I don't want to get into trouble" (Sharon is a hell-raiser when it comes to her baby sister and family in general). So I hung up, shaking my head and smiling because my sister is a bit protective of me, so I kind of understood his reluctance. It was just surprising that Kelvin had to think about who to call first (smiling).

About ten minutes later, my mom called and heard me sounding like myself and said, "Kelvin said you would sound like LaShawn."

I chuckled and said, "Yes, ma'am!" She talked to me for a little while, and I told her that God gave this to me for a reason, I don't know why or what He has in store for me, but there's a reason. I told her not to worry because I was going to beat this because God has the wheel. I was only thirty-four years old, and I have a long life to live, and I need to see my babies grow up. So this was not going to stop me because I had things to do. She said she was glad to hear that, they (her and my dad) would be down in the morning. I know deep down that Mommy knew I was a fighter anyway!

After about five minutes or so, the phone started ringing, ringing, ringing, and ringing and would not stop. My family started calling me, crying. I asked them, in a panicked voice, what was wrong. They would reply you. I told them to stop crying because I would be all right. Meanwhile I thought I was the one with the cancer, not them, so why were they crying! I just stayed strong no matter what! Answering the phone normally and letting them cry or do what they needed to do because we were going to fight this together, so they needed to let it out so we could get to work. I never underestimated my faith in God that He would have me succumb to this cancer. I was going to beat this and fast. I just had to follow God's plan and not want to lead (leadership skills).

The third silent fight within my soul was one disappointing event during my remission process when I wrecked my 2007 Yukon Denali XL into two parked cars and dismantled a fire hydrant after blacking out while driving on pain medicine, psychotic medicine, and chemo pills on January 24, 2010. I had started working to bring in more money and to help with my memory. You're probably asking yourself, why were you behind the wheel of a moving vehicle under the influence of prescription medication? I cannot answer that because I don't remember. I do remember coming to and seeing all the airbags deployed and not having a scratch on me. God watches over babies and fools! I was a fool that day by driving myself around. I also remember calling Kelvin on the car phone, but I think he did not answer because I was going to tell him I did not feel well. Instead I came to, looking around and seeing a car pushed into the median which was on a side street, a car that was sideswiped on the curb, and the fire hydrant on the ground with a little water coming out; but all the airbags were deployed, and I wasn't touched. God is an awesome God!

The police came and asked me if I was okay and taking prescription drugs because I looked like I was in a twilight. So he asked me if I could call someone to come and get me, and I said yes, my husband was on his way. Once he arrived, the police officer spoke with him, but I don't know what he had told him because he never said. I did find out that I didn't get a ticket because my truck was tagged that I was a cancer patient (I think). I was blessed because my license could have been revoked or suspended until I was off the medication. However, I don't remember taking any medication that morning. I went to the childcare center I was helping go through accreditation, and they said I was acting funny, and they would have someone take me home after I laid my head on the desk; but I guess I thought I felt better, so I drove. I can't remember if this was the first time I drove myself somewhere or not. I do know that I was working part-time when I felt up to it to stay busy and to keep my mind fresh. I keep asking myself why he allowed me to get behind the wheel. I really don't know. I just assume he thought I was okay to drive by myself. I must have had to call him when I was on my way back home, so he could be waiting for me, just in case I wasn't back home at the designated time, then he knew to come looking for me (being independent). I am assuming this statement because I do not know why I was driving while medicated. I don't know if I ever asked him!

Later that day, I did go to the hospital just to make sure I was okay. They just told me not to drive when I took the medicine. For months, I wondered why he let me drive under those conditions, and

I never remember getting a clear answer from him. I had my loved ones worried. They called me every day to check on me for about three months. They did not want me working because they felt I wasn't ready, but I had a mission. No one could have stopped me from working once I made my mind up (hardheaded).

I do feel a little more overwhelmed now that I am in a different stage in my life, but not so that I would change anything. Yes, to my family, I may have changed because I don't want them to depend on me; but I am still LaShawn, just all grown-up now and wanting to live my life for me. I may make mistakes along the way, but they are mine, not anyone else's. We are supposed to make mistakes, just if we take them as a learning experience and try not to keep making the same ones repeatedly. I do believe things happen for a reason and just because it has a different face may not mean it's a different situation. We must see things with our eyes wide open first before we introduce our mind, body, and soul.

The disease did not kill me, my faulty marriage hasn't torn me down, and my God hasn't given up on me, so I have another opportunity to make my life what it should be (filled with happiness). I know every day will not be a perfect day, but if I wake up, I am going to make the best out of it. Thinking back on all the obstacles I was faced with, and I still came through victorious, all I can do is praise Him! Remembering that on December 10, 2008, the initial doctor only gave me two years to live, and I am now going into my twelfth year of being cancer-free. I serve nothing but an awesome God!

Anymore it seems like every day is a challenge of some kind for me. If it's not physical, it's psychological, or it's something I just can't really explain. It's very strange how it happens, though, just out of nowhere. I can't help but think it's a sign, but what kind of sign and for whom? I am glad I do not have a set schedule or routine because it is always changing in some manner or capacity. Children and life have a way of working itself out for me, in my own manner, for some reason. I know it can only be through the Holy Spirit. Don't get me wrong, I have been feeling good about everything going on in my life, but I have noticed that my children make me a stressor/worrier. I spend so much time trying to make sure I am providing the best parenting I know how that I sometimes forget that pushing them will not make them be what I want them to be because they have their own minds. All I can do is make sure I am there if they fall and protect them from things I know will hurt them.

As a rape victim, cancer survivor, congestive heart failure survivor, divorcée, and psychological survivor (memory coming back), I can see that believing in a higher power has moved many mountains out of my way because I try to live by the Word. I don't always do or say the right things, but I try to live as an example of how strong my faith is if you just believe. I am finding that if you truly let go and let God, your life and situations will change no matter what the cost, but you have to really let go of all the things that are blocking you from letting him in 100 percent.

When you are a person with many dreams and high standards, it's hard not to be a silent fighter. There are many situations and obstacles you must face just to make it through and to gain respect. My mission is to always fight for what I want because no one can fight for me. They can fight with me, but ultimately it is my fight. As I mature, I see that I have strong, resilient, and optimistic characteristics which make me a diamond for fighting a good fight that no one else can see. It has made me realize that it's nothing but faith that helps me be resilient to keep surviving, and it is giving me the will to learn how to cope.

LEARNING HOW TO COPE

*Thinking should become your capital Asset no matter
ups and downs you come across in your life.*

—A. P. J Abdul Kalama

When you think about coping, there may be many facets to your coping mechanism. Learning how to cope is not as easy as one may think because your physical, emotional, spiritual, and psychological factors must be considered. It is no different for me! I hid the way in which I coped most of my life because I did not want you to really understand who I was/am and try to make assumptions. As the statement goes, "assuming can make an ass out of you." For the most part, that is very true! I recently realized that if you are not understood, you carry burdens you don't have to because you will have someone to talk to. Therefore, if you don't know me, you will never understand me nor be able to cope with who I am. Since I very seldom let you in (trust), learning how to cope for me has its challenges. First, I must observe who you are and what you stand for in my life. Then I must feel relaxed (not too relaxed) when you tell me things. Next I analyze the process in which things occurred to see if there is a need for me to even entertain the situation. Somehow I come up with a logical theory (I won't reveal) which only I can figure out to make a valid and accurate analysis of how I will cope with the situation where my character is not jeopardized. Finally I am always who I say I am no matter what the circumstance (I never try to be something I am not) because there are too many obstacles and people involved to have to remember who you are in any given moment. Nevertheless, I have way too much and many things I had to consider in my life which added to how I would cope with my situations. Let me tell you, if I let you in my life, I have a very good reason, unless my higher power has already given you instructions (diligence). Another thing, if you are let in my world, please cherish it because if you do one thing, you will be out and not even considered a thought to me (coping without representation). I am not a difficult person, but I cherish the people, circumstances, power, blessings, and job I have been given to be able to explain how I cope or how I can learn how to cope with everyone even family.

So learning how to cope with myself because my life was constantly changing in so many ways challenged my own theory. I not only had to deal with myself for answers, but I had others who looked to me for answers which placed a great powerful image in my mind and on my thoughts. I had children, career adjustment, failing marriage, and health issues now that added to my coping mechanism. Believe it or not, how I cope determines the outcome of all my new situations. See, early on in life, I knew there was always something different about me. Some could see it, but most could not. It wasn't a cover-up in no shape, form, or fashion; it was just me being me. So the more mature and wise I became, the more coping strategies I had to encounter. I had to cope with things internally before I could even comprehend the external factors. I was taught (blessed) to be very, very, very independent, and my challenge would be coping with people helping me as I grow and move forward in my life.

My reality was becoming my normal! I had to start thinking about more than just myself and coping with that was a high demand itself. I held strong leadership qualities, but when it comes to your personal life, that doesn't always help with learning how to cope with life's challenges/ situations. It's time to take one thing at a time and conquer that before moving to another situation because my previous situation's outcome can determine how I cope with the rest. This is my maturing thoughts and circumstances coming along once again. See, I can tell you that learning how to cope just comes from life's experiences, but there is so much more to it that only you can figure it out. Yes, we have people who study these things and provide strategies for us, but each of us are unique so we can't treat or cope with things the same way or even treat situations which are the same in the same manner because things change and people change. It has taken me years to figure this out, and I am still trying to figure it out, but I take one day at a time which helps me a lot.

So as I am going through my struggles, I notice that the way in which I cope will alter the way in which the situation takes flight. The ball is in my hand, and I must treat it like I am a professional with little to no previous skill. A crazy way of thinking, but it helps me (smiling)! Today, I must have a sense of humor because coping with some people, places, things, situations, and overall experiences can break me down, and I'm not ready to lose no fight. For the most part, my steady coping mechanism started with my career, finances, and personal life. When I decided to make drastic changes, I also had to decide how I was going to learn how to cope with the changes. My main concern was with my children because they have not been on earth long enough to own up to what society has in store for them. I must fight for them as much as I can. Yes, they have a father, but the mother is always supposed to handle her children, I believe. As the saying goes, "Mommy babies, Daddys maybes." Well, they are his children, but I had to carry them inside of me for nine months, and I will have to continue that process for the rest of their lives; so I had to change the way I coped with situations and my thinking processes.

Shortly after Kayla was born, it changed for my marriage. However, after Layden was born, it started to reveal its head more frequently. I needed to become even more focused on my future with or without him. I needed to be there for my children no matter what, and the way I cope with it is a major factor. This was very new to me, and learning how to cope with it was going to take time. I am a planner, organizer, or just an overall perfectionist, but I can't do that right now when I have other people to consider. I was changing/maturing! The first thing I did for my children was secure future finances for them by opening up savings accounts for them and putting money aside for a rainy day. I want them to go to college, and it is going to cost, so I need to be ready. He and I were having problems, so I knew he would be of little to no help when it came to the future of the children. However, he really didn't know what he wanted to do with his life nor where he would be so him helping me was questionable. Now he would talk like he was going to help, but his actions said something different. It was time to go into mommy mode and do what I needed to do for all the children. I was working hard and feeling burnt out. This was when our lives really turned (marriage failure thoughts arose). I had to make an agenda, and I had to stick to it no matter what (stressor). Unfortunately I did not have time to wait on him or anyone else when it came to my children. I was the mother, so I had to do the sacrificing. This is not the way it should be, though! When you are married or have children together, you should both be willing to sacrifice for them and cope with the situation as one, not two. Regrettably that's not always how life goes for many of us.

I always looked at life from a glass window, I think. On the outside looking in! But now, there is no window to hide behind, it's just me. So as I was traveling along in my life, it suddenly hit me that, *LaShawn, you are the key! LaShawn, you are the common denominator!* Wow, now that was a tough one to swallow for me. How will I cope with this and what learning tools am I going to need (surprised and shocked all at the same time)?

When I was going through my illness and separation, oh my, how I had to learn how to cope quickly. I started noticing actions speak louder than words in so many instances. Regretfully Marilyn was at the root of it all for me, in my eyes. She should have kept her mouth shut the day we went shopping for shoes, and she noticed him staring (smiling). I did not move to DC for a man, and I could see he was the type of person who talked a good game but very seldom carried it out for one reason or another, and I did not have time for games. Life was getting serious, and I had to cope with situations I never thought I would have to face. I needed his support right now, if I never needed it before (tears). It just wasn't there! Now how do I learn how to cope with that on my mind? With a heavy heart, I knew I would be on my own with raising my children and preparing for my children's future. All this coping strategy while also trying to get my health back on track. Just getting stronger physically and mentally, period! I was very blessed to be getting stronger physically, but I had a lot of work to do for myself mentally. I can honestly admit that my mental state was not very healthy! It saddens me to say that or even think it, but it's so true (dangerous).

I had to do something! Since I was becoming a little stronger physically every day, I took on some part-time work to start putting my goals in order. I am nothing but a fighter! I knew I had to wait to make it to my fifth-year anniversary of being in remission to be off permanent disability and could work full-time. Although once you have a terminal illness, you never fully recover no matter how hard you try. Yes, you can cover it up from the outside world, but inside, you are usually a walking time bomb, ready to collapse at any given time; but you have the cards in your hand. So I decided that when my five years are up, I am going to go back on my grind for my children, and nothing will stand in my way. Let me say, I did make a decent amount of money on Social Security, but it was not enough to send my children to college and take care of my everyday responsibilities. God got me through!

At first, it was hard because I really did not know if I had the energy to go back to work full-time or consistently at that point. I just knew I had to get back to work! No, the doctors did not want me to jump right back into it with full force, but I had to do what I had to do and staying stress-free was very hard emotionally for me. I cried many a days! By God's grace and my faith, I was blessed to have gotten some help with the children from Marilyn and my daughter's friend's dad, LaRone. Let me tell you, LaRone has been my saving grace on many occasions, and he doesn't even know it. I want to publicly *thank* him for having such a gracious heart for my children. Marilyn loves my children so much she would do anything for them, and I publicly *thank* her as well! I was starting to recognize I did know a little more than I thought about how I was going to cope. I put my life and situation in the hands of God and left them there. I just follow His lead *all* the time! I don't even question it either!

Amazingly with LaRone, he has one child of his own that he is raising alone, but he never hesitated to take both of mine, even though Layden was still in the potty training stage. I joke around with Kirsten, telling her that she thinks she's my third child (grinning). It feels good to have such great people around you who don't ask questions when you need a little helping hand. It makes coping just a little lighter, and your normality to your reality makes a little more sense. LaRone and I really help each other because I help him with his daughter when he needs a woman's perspective. It's a great friendship!

I am glad my daughter has such a great friend with a thoughtful father who doesn't mind helping me out if I need him. I know he has his own way; he must learn how to cope with raising a daughter on his own since she was born. He does have his mother who will help, but I don't think he asks her very often. We are similar in thinking when it comes to our children and asking for help (smiling).

Sidenote: LaRone and I have just become good friends over the years, nothing else, just a great respectable friendship. I know what you were thinking (laughing). We made ourselves family (smiling)! Our children have been friends since the girls were in pre-K together. Kirsten was the only child invited from school for Kayla's birthday party that year who showed up, and they have been friends ever since. They have their disagreements and own personalities, but they still can be friends (my daughter has attitude and Kirsten is talkative). They complement each other is what I tell them. I pray they can remain friends forever because it will be a wonderful thing for both. They can go through things together and still love each other like sisters. This relationship makes my coping a little less stressful.

However, because I have experienced so many obstacles at such a young age (well, I'm not that young)—well, you get it—that learning how to cope is getting just a little easier. I believe once my children are grown, and I really don't have to have contact with their father as much, my coping tactics will be better. Teaching myself to cope with him was a big challenge for me because I was still disappointed in the way he treated me when I was sick. I didn't want to have to cope with his behaviors forever (today I am better coping with him).

I have found, though, that if I have time for me, just me, I can strategize my coping much better. I must find or make time for just me because I can feel my energy melting daily. It is a part of maturing, but managing it is my struggle with certain people and situations. Now that I am divorced and in remission for over eleven years, I can finally start adjusting some of my plans. I still have a long way to go with learning how to cope, but I just take it one day at a time and cherish the friendships I have made throughout.

My circle of friends and family has become part of my strategy for coping because each have a different role in my life and no two are the same. They have really helped me keep a supportive mind. When I can testify that I have support of the mind, then I have found something good that can work for me. As the song goes by Marvin Sapp:

I won't complain;
I've had some good days,
I've had some hills to climb,
I've had some weary days,
I've had some sleepless nights,
But when I look around,
And I think things over,
All of my good days,
Outweigh my bad days;
So I won't complain.
Sometimes the clouds hang low,
I can hardly see the road,
And then I ask the question,
Lord why so much pain,
But He knows what's best for me,
Although my weary eyes can't see,
So I'll just say thank you Lord;
I won't complain.
God's been so good to me,
The Lord has been so good to me,
More than this old world
Or you could ever be,
The Lord has been so good to me,
And He dried my tears away,
And He turn all my midnights into days,
So I'll say thank you Lord;
I just say thank you Lord;
I'll just say thank you Lord;
I won't complain.
(http://www.urbanlyrics.com/lyrics/marvin-winans/iwontcomplain.html)

I can stay prayed up and lifted in the name of Jesus because He ultimately has a plan for me through all the trials and tribulations I have gone through and will continue to go through. My coping strategies and learning how to cope with what I cannot control, even what I think I can control, my situations will become easier. I believe my health, strength, power, and dedication to becoming a greater person today than I was yesterday have all the support of my mind in it.

SUPPORT OF THE MIND

You are strong when you know your weaknesses;
You are beautiful when you appreciate your flaws;
You are wise when you learn from your mistakes.

—Unknown

When it comes to supporting my mind, I had to think about all the situations that I encountered. My mind is only as strong as my weakest link! Therefore, while going through my ordeal, I had a really difficult time letting go and having to depend on family and close friends to take care of me. So while I was going to chemotherapy, I began seeing a psychiatrist and psychologist for therapy to help me cope with understanding that I had to depend on people in order for me to get better. These individuals were not looking at me, feeling sorry for me, but for emotional and physical support.

I am a very private person and do not accept pity for anything or from anyone. I learned that when I was diagnosed and couldn't even wash myself, I had a problem with it. I went through weekly sessions while going through my chemo treatments at the hospital. Most of the sessions, I would be crying because I had to learn to accept help and not to think of it negatively. I was very emotional, and I just kept thinking, *Who are you, LaShawn?* I thought I was weak because all I would do was cry as I was talking about my past and present situations. I was very vulnerable! I was carrying a lot of things inside that I never wanted to reveal, so I put up a wall so I didn't have to let anyone in if I didn't want to. Now I had no choice but to open up!

This was very difficult for me! I had to face my own reality as not normal or a failure. Once I figured out that letting go helps build a better character and have more strength, I was all right. It did not happen overnight, and I did not want to talk about everything. I only wanted to work with the situation at hand and my future. My past hurt too much to talk about it because I had demons and skeletons that I asserted I'd never talk about. They aren't anything that would kill me, but it could taint my character I built up thus far. It's more of my own demons that I face because I have lots of regrets and forgiveness that I don't necessarily want to let go. I know everyone has skeletons, and mine aren't any different, they are just things I want to be left alone. Unfortunately therapists, psychologists, and psychiatrists try their best to get these things out of you so you can free your mind, but I just believe I can't change them so why talk about them? It is what it is!

Since I still had things I needed to let go, I continued seeing a therapist at Dr. Cephas' office in Takoma Park, Maryland, in August 2009, until December 2015. Let me say this too, individuals who enjoy messing with one's minds are the most difficult to work with (future psychologist). My sessions continued weekly, but as I began allocating the situations in my life differently, they decreased to once a month. Honestly, I decreased the visit because I really was getting tired of feeling like I was even more dysfunctional when I left. It didn't seem as if I was really getting the help I needed by talking to a therapist. I was so all over the place with my emotions that they had prescribed me medication for anxiety, depression, and sleeping because I was not sleeping. I always had problems sleeping, but getting no sleep at all was not good for my health. They told me my mind was constantly moving and because I felt I was having memory loss, I was overexerting my brain (funny). How can you overexert your brain? I guess I was doing too much (smiling).

In my mind, I had to exceed my daily limit of thinking because I wanted to still do the things I used to do with no problem. I was using my mind in a capacity that could have resulted in a major destruction. That did not even concern me because I was willing to take that chance. I needed my critical thinking skills to function as they were to free up some space in my mind for new things. I was taking on more responsibilities, and I needed to be able to think clearly. The psychiatrist warned me that if I continued to go beyond my brain capacity that I may never be able to gain any of my temporary memory that I lost again. They even said that if I did not slow down, it could possibly interfere with my long-term memory over time. I just blanked them out and put it in God's hands. In my mind, the memory loss was only diagnosed as temporary because I had been through a traumatic experience in which temporary memory loss was not uncommon. So I decided to let things happen and try not to stress about it because I did not want any of my memory to be lost forever. I had already lost most of my childhood memories because my brother was killed when I was eight years old, and Sharon moved so I felt lonely, but no one ever knew because I just wouldn't say anything. I believed showing emotions was a sign of feebleness. I don't believe anyone told me that it was just something I believed because it was easier to cope with life's disappointments. If you train your mind, body, and soul to react a certain way, then you get accustomed to it.

It seemed like my life was a blur the whole year (2009). I was just going through the motions but not really knowing which way I was going. I was following God's plan, and He was in total control. So I overlooked a lot of things that did not relate to any of my needs. He and I were going through things that I felt would not be happening if I had not been sick and weak. It felt like all the work I put into trying to save a marriage I really was out of in 2005 but still wanted to somehow save face for others turned into nothing. I didn't want my children growing up with their parents divorced and having split visitation into two households. I knew Kayla loved her daddy, and I didn't want to destroy that. Layden's bond was different because he barely had a relationship with him anyway. But never wanted to leave Bryan and Bria with him if I could help it, but by this time, they were grown.

Since I didn't have a close relationship with my dad until I got grown and had a child of my own, even though he lived with me, I wanted that for my children, especially Kayla. I was always a momma's girl, but I think not having that closeness or being Daddy's princess affected me, and I did not want that for Kayla (my dad shows his love a different way, and I am okay with that today!). So I would sacrifice my happiness so they could have a normal life. No one knew about anything I was doing, not even him. But once I was diagnosed with cancer, I knew, deep down inside, it was because of stress and the pressure of not wanting a failed marriage since I had already done things I never wanted to experience even as a little girl.

So at my last heart doctor's appointment in October 2010, they told me that my heart rate had improved with no damage and that I only had to take the medication if I needed it. I didn't need to be monitored as frequently, only if there was a problem. I had no mishaps after this period, which could only be God's miracle working again. My faith helped to bring me through with God's saving grace. I knew it was time! I had no choice but to make some life-changing decisions, and the first one was to end this faulty marriage I tried so hard to save just to save face. I was so miserable inside this marriage that I believe it was killing me slowly. As my quote at the beginning states, *"You are strong when you know your weaknesses; You are beautiful when you appreciate your flaws; You are wise when you learn from your mistakes."* This is all I had been going through for over thirteen years, and I had to hit rock bottom to figure it out. Never again will I let that happen to me! My mind is precious as well as my health and strength, so if I had to leave an energy-driven, untrustworthy, egotistic marriage, that was just what I was going to do.

I had to start thinking for the support of my sanity and well-being. No one cares more about you than you. Unfortunately I had to learn that the hard way! My sanity is more important than being in a relationship that is going to kill me mentally, emotionally, psychologically, and spiritually. I am determined to fight a good fight and make sure my mind is prepared to lead and learn. I had to face a challenge that I never thought would eventually make me terminally ill before I found strength to take that leap. Sometimes God puts you in places you have never seen just to see how you will turn out. Even if it's for the good and sometimes if it's for the bad. In the end, it is all to make you open your eyes, see what's in front of you, and if it is in your best mindset, then leave it alone. Don't ever sacrifice your mental circumstances for others' gratification! Keep your eyes open, even when you want to close them because there is always something to be seen that your mind may not be able to support. We have to fight a good fight in order to win!

FIGHTING A GOOD FIGHT TO WIN

*The struggle you're in today is developing
the strength you need for tomorrow.*

—Unknown Author

On January 14, 2009, I was in remission; I was cancer-free. All I could say was thank you, Jesus! So now I was ready to start my chemo treatments to kill and prevent any trace of the cancerous cells in my body. The treatment I was going to receive was studied in Japan and had a high success rate in patients with APL. Although I was a special case because I was black, young, and female, they did not treat me any differently. I think there was great concern of the outcome it could have on me, but God was in control, so there was never anything to be concerned with in my eyes and heart. So while I was sent home with ATRA chemo pills, I would come back in about a week or so to begin my IV chemo treatment. Consequently when I was discharged from the hospital, they gave me the prescription for ATRA because I had to continue taking those right away. As I stated earlier, this prescription being filled was a nightmare. I had to take four pills three times a day for one and a half years which meant I would be taking them until July 2010. I would start my arsenic treatment on January 26, 2009, and ended on April 24, 2009. These dates may be a little different, but the treatment was five days a week for five weeks with two weeks off, then back for five days a week for five more weeks. I would finish with a biopsy to make sure all the cancer was out.

I received my first treatment on Monday, January 26, 2009. I was receiving a chemo named arsenic trioxide through my PICC line. This chemo is used to treat all acute promyelocytic leukemia (APL) patients. I was very nervous but gracious at the same time because my God is in the healing business, and I am His patient now; so I thought to myself, *Take the wheel, Lord, and leave this old body behind so I can open myself up to a new one you have created just for me, amen.* This became my daily prayer before each treatment because I did not know if the doctors had confidence that it would even work for me because they had never had to treat a patient of African descent before.

According to Chemocare.com, 2015:

Arsenic Trioxide is an anti-cancer ("antineoplastic" or "cytotoxic") chemotherapy drug. This medication is classified as a "natural product." Arsenic trioxide is used to treat a specific type (the leukemia cells must show an alteration in their genetic makeup when examined in the laboratory) of acute promyelocytic leukemia (APL) when retinoid or anthracycline chemotherapy has not been effective. It may also be used for multiple myeloma, chronic myelogenous leukemia, and acute myelogenous leukemia.

Arsenic trioxide is administered into a vein (intravenous, IV) over the course of one or two hours over a consecutive number of days. This may be extended up to four hours if the patient has a vasomotor reaction (lightheadedness, change in blood pressure). The amount of arsenic trioxide that you will receive depends on many factors, including your height and weight, your general health or other health problems, and the type of cancer or condition being treated. Your doctor will determine your dose and schedule.

The following side effects are common (occurring in greater than 30%) for patients taking arsenic trioxide: nausea and vomiting, cough, fatigue, fever, headache, rapid heartbeats (tachycardia), abdominal pain, diarrhea, shortness of breath, blood test abnormalities (low potassium and magnesium) (elevated blood glucose level) (some refer to this as "sugar"), swelling of the face, hands, feet or legs (edema), sore throat, difficulty sleeping (insomnia), rash, heart rhythm changes (seen on EKG tests), joint pain, itching, numbness or tingling of hands or feet, chills, and anxiety

These side effects are less common side effects (occurring in about 10–29%) of patients receiving arsenic trioxide: constipation, chest pain, low blood pressure, poor appetite, nosebleeds or bruising, depression, muscle, bone or generalized pains, dizziness, post nasal drip or sinusitis, altered blood liver enzyme levels, low blood counts: white and red blood cells and platelets may temporarily decrease causing an increased risk for infection, anemia and/or bleeding, blood count abnormalities (high potassium level), weight gain, vaginal bleeding, and dry skin.

A **very serious side effect** that is preventable with proper monitoring and immediate treatment is APL differentiation syndrome. This syndrome is a reaction between the drug and the leukemia. This syndrome produces fever, difficulty breathing, and weight gain and lung and heart problems. It is generally treated with high-dose steroids. In most cases, treatment with arsenic trioxide will continue.

Some self-care tips to follow: drink at least two to three quarts of fluid every 24 hours, unless you are instructed otherwise; avoid crowds or people with colds; wash your hands often; use a soft toothbrush, and rinse three times a day with 1/2 to 1 teaspoon of baking soda and/or 1/2 to 1 teaspoon of salt mixed with 8 ounces of water; use an electric razor and a soft toothbrush to minimize bleeding; avoid contact sports or activities that could cause injury; take anti-nausea medications as prescribed by your doctor, and eat small, frequent meals; avoid *sun exposure by wearing SPF 15 (or higher) sun-block and protective clothing; drinking alcoholic beverages should be kept to a minimum or avoided completely; get plenty of rest; and maintain good nutrition.*

Arsenic-containing preparations have been in medical use for more than 2000 years. Arsenic-based therapy was used in the United States and Europe more than 100 years ago to treat leukemia and infections, but modern chemotherapy and anti-biotics replaced these treatments. More recently, interest in arsenic-based therapy was revived by reports of the anti-leukemic activity of some tradi-tional Chinese preparations. Chinese scientists sub-sequently found out that the active ingredient was arsenic trioxide.

I had to endure ten weeks of chemotherapy and take the ATRA for one and a half years to be totally cleared and have no recurrences. This was the treatment plan for every patient who is diagnosed with APL. If it will totally cure me, I will do what I must do. I had total faith that the Lord would put his touch on the diagnoses, and I would stay cured with little to no difficulties. I just had to follow the rules and not vary for one second. I was the follower and leader all at the same time during this stage of my cancer recovery.

After my second week of treatments, I started getting a knot in my right forearm (which was the arm my PICC line was in). It was hurting so bad, and I was getting nervous. I called the hospital and they instructed me to go to the emergency room immediately. Thus my mom took me back to UMMC's ER in Baltimore to have it checked. They ran some tests and discovered it was a blood clot formed from the PICC line. The doctors had to get in touch with my doctor before they could remove it. We got to the hospital around 10:00 p.m. on Friday and did not leave until 8:00 a.m. on Saturday, waiting for them to tell us what they were going to do about the line. My mom fell asleep sitting up in the chair, but I stayed awake, worrying about them keeping me. I did not want to be admitted again, oh no!

The doctor came in around 6:00 a.m. and said my doctor had called and informed them that they could remove it. I had to stay and be monitored for about one and a half hours before being discharged. What a relief when they instructed me that I did not have to take any medicine because it would heal on its own since the line was out (praise God!). When I initially received the PICC line, they said I would have to keep it in for at least eighteen months. I needed the lines for me to receive my chemo treatment which was three at a time in some cases.

However, that Monday when I returned for my third week of chemo treatment, they sent me to have a PICC line put in my left arm. This doctor did not seem to be gentle or friendly at all. He did not give me any instructions nor warnings to what was going to happen. He put the line in even though I was telling him my arm was hurting. He acted like he had no heart or feelings about how much pain I was in from this line. I kept thinking he put it in wrong. This time, my arm was sore for two weeks, and I had to continue getting treatments in it. Every time you touched it, a sharp pain went up my arm. It was so excruciating I could not stand it! I had to keep this thing in for fifteen or sixteen months; it was not going to happen because I was miserable and pain meds weren't doing anything.

I stayed strong and positive because I knew I only had a short time to go. But on March 13, 2009, my blood pressure had dropped tremendously, and I had severe diarrhea. So they had to take this line out and give me a temporary one because I was admitted into the ICU. It had gotten infected again, and now I was very, very sick. I didn't know what was going on for real.

When I got to the ICU floor, they had this hot bright light shining down on me, and the team of nurses were stripping my clothes off. They took off everything, even my wedding ring and earrings. It was so bad because I was alert and could have taken off my own clothes. I wasn't delusional, so I could have communicated with them. I guess it was protocol in the ICU when a patient comes in with something life threatening, you treat them all like they are trauma patients. They just continued to undress me even though I was talking. I felt so violated in a way because six women stripped me down, in less than five minutes, from head to toe. I remember the nurse practitioner Julie telling them that I was alert, but they kept on with their protocol.

Kelvin was with me that day! I was in infusion receiving treatment when this happened, so they just transported me upstairs. That was a very impersonal experience that day! He really looked concerned because when he left me, I was fine. He came back, and I was in the bathroom for about an hour; so the nurse came and knocked on the door, but I had diarrhea so bad that I couldn't get up. Once I came out, that's when all the action started! I received another PICC line but in my neck this time so I could get numerous medications at once. I had bacteria in the line which caused this sudden reaction. They gave me some antibiotics and pain medication to clear it up. I was in the ICU for about a week, and they transferred me to the cancer unit for three days. I don't think anyone could stay with me in the ICU, so I had to stick those stays out by myself. This happened during the Easter holiday in 2009. Sharon came when they moved me to the cancer floor where I was for three more days which went into my Monday treatment. So I had to wait an extra day in infusion to get all the doses of the treatment I needed.

After that episode, I had to have my heart checked every day with an EKG machine which was in the hospital on the third floor. I had to make sure it came back good before I could even get treatment. I had to walk down two hallways to the elevator, to the third floor, then walk down another hallway to the EKG room. It took me about fifteen to twenty minutes to walk and have the procedure. I did this alone every day! When Sharon found that out, she was furious! I did not think anything of it because it was just my routine now. Since I had five more weeks of treatment, I would have to get another PICC line back in my right arm. I was just not having any luck with these PICC lines!

Now this one really, really hurt, and halfway through the second cycle, it stopped working. Now I was back in the hospital for Mother's Day because my arm was infected again. This time, they did not give me another line because I only had a week or so left. So they gave me a single line that had to be changed every three days. That was better than my arms throbbing all day and night in pain. This hospital stay was another five days. Marcia told me that she was not celebrating any more holidays because I was always ending up in the hospital. I could not even say anything (smiling).

While going through these treatments, he took me most of the time, but Sharon, my mom, and my niece Shayna went with me a few times. Each time I went, I took a blanket so that I could go to sleep while receiving my treatment. At first, I was taking a journal to write my experiences in, but during the second cycle, I had to work on Kayla's project for DARE, a program that gives students a computer and software to help them in school up to sixth grade. She was only in preschool, but I wanted her to try and win. She said she wanted to be an astronaut when she grew up, so I designed a space-ship with a black Barbie astronaut and all the things she would need if she went up in space. She won first place and was the youngest to enter and win. Kayla was the only student to ever enter and win from Francis Scott Key Elementary School in District Heights, Maryland. This was a huge honor!

Since I was taking pain medicine to relieve some of the pain I was having from the biopsy and treatment, my doctor told me that I was taking too much medicine, so she referred me to UMMC pain clinic. Once there, they looked at my charts and took some blood and agreed I was in much pain. At first, I was just given higher doses of the pain medicine I was on, but after a while, it wasn't working. I especially needed it for the biopsy I would be getting for the next three years. So every three months, I would go to the pain clinic and have my SI joints burned and steroids so I could withstand some of the pain right before the biopsy procedure. My parents would come and take me.

The SI joints are a *sacroiliac (SI) joint injection—also called a sacroiliac joint block—is primarily used either to diagnose or treat low back pain and/or sciatica symptoms associated with sacroiliac joint dysfunction.*

The sacroiliac joints lie next to the spine and connect the sacrum with the hip on both sides. There are two sacroiliac joints, one on the right and one on the left. Joint inflammation and/or dysfunction in this area can cause pain. Read more about Sacroiliac Joint Dysfunction.

The purpose of a sacroiliac joint injection old: to diagnose the source of a patient's pain, and to provide therapeutic pain relief. At times, these are separated, and a patient will undergo a purely diagnostic or therapeutic injection, although often the two are combined into one injection.

1. Diagnosis

2. *A diagnostic SI joint injection is used to confirm a suspected diagnosis of sacroiliac joint dysfunction. This is done by numbing the sacroiliac joint with local anesthetic (e.g. lidocaine). The injection is performed under fluoroscopy (X-ray guidance) for accuracy. Once the needle has entered the sacroiliac joint, contrast is injected into the joint to ensure proper needle placement and proper spread of medication. The numbing medication is then injected into the joint.*

3. *After the numbing medication is injected, the patient is asked to try and reproduce the pain by performing normally painful activities. If the patient experiences 75–80% pain relief for the normal duration of the anesthetic, a tentative diagnosis of SI joint dysfunction is made. A second diagnostic sacroiliac injection should be performed using a different numbing medication (e.g. Bupivicaine) in order to confirm the diagnosis.*

If this second diagnostic injection also provides 75–80% pain relief for the duration of the anesthetic, there is a reasonable degree of medical certainty the sacroiliac joint is the source of the patient's pain.

Some practitioners are performing lateral branch blocks to diagnose SI joint pain. The lateral branch nerves are small nerves that branch off the sacral spinal nerves and provide sensation to the joint. A lateral branch block might be performed to determine if a patient is a candidate for a **radiofrequency nerve ablation** *to provide longer lasting relief of the pain associated with SI joint dysfunction.*

4. Pain Relief

5. *A therapeutic SI joint injection is done to provide relief of the pain associated with sacroiliac joint dysfunction. The injection is performed using the same technique as a diagnostic SI joint injection, except that anti-inflammatory medication (corticosteroid) is included in the injection to provide pain relief by reducing inflammation within the joint.*

6. *If the patient experiences prolonged pain relief after a therapeutic sacroiliac joint injection, he or she can begin a* **physical therapy and rehabilitation program** *to further reduce pain and return the patient to normal activity levels.*

7. *If the therapeutic sacroiliac joint injection is successful in reducing or eliminating the patient's pain for a longer duration, it may be repeated up to three times per year, in conjunction with physical therapy and rehabilitation program, to help the patient maintain normal function.*

The Sacroiliac Joint injection procedure is usually performed in an operating room or a dedicated procedure room. The entire procedure usually takes only minutes, and the patient goes home the same day.

The following outlines the typical injection procedure:

- *After informed consent has been obtained, the patient lies face down on his or her stomach on the radiography table. A pillow might be placed under the hips for patient comfort.*
- *The patient's vitals (e.g. pulse rate and blood pressure) are monitored throughout the procedure.*
- *Depending on the physician and the patient's preference, an intravenous line may be inserted to deliver medication to help the patient relax.*
- *To maintain sterility, the skin overlying the sacroiliac joint injection is cleansed using an iodine based solution (e.g. Povidine-Iodine) or an alcohol-based antiseptic (e.g. chlorhexidine 0.5% in 70% alcohol). Sterile gloves are used throughout the entire injection procedure.*
- *For the patient's comfort, the needle insertion site is often numbed using local anesthetic. Once the needle enters the sacroiliac joint under fluoroscopy guidance, contrast—"dye" that shows up under X-ray—is injected to verify needle placement within the sacroiliac joint and to verify spread of solution within the joint.*
- *Once the needle has been guided into the joint successfully, diagnostic and/or therapeutic medications are injected into the joint.*
- *Two types of medications are typically injected:*
  - *A local anesthetic (usually lidocaine or bupivacaine) is typically injected into the joint with the goal of determining immediate pain relief to confirm the sacroiliac joint as the source of the patient's pain. This*

solution is used for a diagnostic sacroiliac joint injection.

o *An anti-inflammatory medication (usually a corticosteroid) may help reduce inflammation within the joint, which in turn could help alleviate the pain over a longer period of time (typically for several months, up to a year). This solution is injected for a therapeutic sacroiliac joint injection.*
(Veritashealth.com 2015)

My treatment was over, and it was time for another biopsy on June 1, 2009. The result came back negative for leukemia, so I was still in remission. I was on my way to recovery! Dr. Baer stressed that I could not get pregnant so I asked him if he would get a vasectomy since I had been through all the chemo incidences. Plus he already had two children from a previous marriage, and we had Kayla and Layden, so why not? He said he would do it, but when the time came, he decided he did not want to do it because he already went through a surgery when he was an adult. He stated he wasn't getting cut on again! On September 29, 2009, I had a tubal ligation because I could not get pregnant while on chemo. I didn't want any more children, so it wasn't a big decision for me. The surgery was in and out, and the gynecologist went through my belly button to tie them, so I did not have any scares. I was in a little pain but not too bad. The gynecologist even took pictures of how easy it was to give me, but I did not want them. I thought, *Why would anyone want to keep that!* She just put them in my records!

My parents took me to all my SI joint appointments and all but one of my biopsy procedures. Well, the one time they did not take me, Sharon and Kelvin took me. This was a very different atmosphere to say the least. My parents would usually just sit there quietly and watch to make sure everything was okay. Sharon—oh no—she had to be up close and personal when she went. She stood right by my left side where I turned my head so I didn't have to see the instruments, but I kept my head straight with my arms folded under my chin that day since she was standing on that side. She was rubbing my back, trying to comfort me. Kelvin was just sitting on the chair, by the door, where they always put chairs.

Oh my, once they started the procedure, Sharon started giving me play-by-play of what they were getting ready to do, when they were going to do it, and the instruments they used for each step. I couldn't believe she was giving me play-by-play (shaking my head). She was sounding like she was intrigued! I never wanted to know what the instruments looked like because I know I probably would either move when you told me a step or would be so petrified I would not want it done. Oh, this did not matter to Sharon on this day; she thought she was doing me a favor. Through the entire thirty-minute procedure, she is telling me step by step! I just couldn't believe it! I think from that day forward, all I could do during the procedure is think about her giving me play-by-play (smiling). Only Sharon would do this to me! He was just sitting on the chair behind us, shaking his head. I think he thought, *Wow, Sharon, you really had to give her play-by-play.* Our sense of humor was always questionable with him. After the procedure was over, Sharon said, "I can't believe you could lie there and not move. I would have been trying to watch" (shaking my head).

I said, "Well, I really don't have a choice because one movement would cause me more headaches." I think she told everyone (disbelief but funny).

She just kept saying, "You're a strong chick to sit through that!"

I thought, *Well, if I'm not, you guys are going to be ego tripping* (didn't say it out loud, though). This was the only time she had to go with me because she had to work. My parents continued taking me the rest of the times I needed the procedure. The next one, my dad asked, "Do you keep going in the same spot because she is in a lot of pain when she leaves here."

NP Mike replied, "No, it's just around the same area because we need to get into her hip bone to get the bone marrow." My dad did not look convinced at all (smiling).

The procedures time line went as such: first year, every three months biopsy (2009); second year, every three months biopsy and

SI joint procedure (2010); third year, every three months then, every four months and SI joint procedure (2011); fourth year, every four months and SI joint procedure (2012); fifth year, every six months (2013); and after my fifth year, only once a year for a checkup. My last bone marrow biopsy was on June 24, 2012, because when I went back for my results in December 2012, Dr. Baer said that I did not have to have any more biopsy procedures because I was doing well, and they would only be needed to continue if my blood work came back suspicious. Oh, how I wanted to do the "Holy Ghost" dance right in the middle of that doctor's exam room (smiling). I couldn't believe it (shaking my head). No more agony, no more pain! I had to tell everyone how blessed I had been to have been cured so quickly. This was all for the love of family!

LOVE THY FAMILY

*The things you are passionate about are
not random, they are your calling.*

—Fabiennen Frederickson

I speak a lot about my family. My family really has a special place in my heart. See, not everyone can say they love their family God has given them, but I can truly say it. Yes, we may have our disagreements or differences of opinions, but we still love each other. I never really realized how much love I have for my family and they have for me until the day I found out I was ill. The outpouring of love that my family gave me was incredible. It was an outpour of love from miles away that gave me even more strength to fight my fight. Oh yes, we all have a fight we will have to take, and the support you receive will be your anchor to push on even when you think you have no more strength to move.

The love of my family is phenomenal. We have a bond that little can break no matter how hard they try. I just remember as a little girl, my mom saying, "Don't let no one or nothing tear this family apart, no matter what! We are all family, and we are going to stay a family."

I never fully understood that when I was a little girl, but now that I am a woman with my own children, I understand completely. See, with such a large family, we can sometimes let outside people, situations, or things influence our commitment to the ones that will do anything in the world for us. My mom never wanted that for us, and she strives for us to remain a close-bonded family, even though we all have our own families. Our family is continually growing, and that just gives us the opportunity to teach them how much love we have and share with each other on a regular basis. Sometimes it's a struggle for some of us, but the ones who grew up under my mom's care knows what it means to be family and are expected to teach their children about the importance of staying a family.

So when I became sick, it was natural that everyone was calling and checking on me; although it was somewhat of a surprise that I had an influence on so many of my family's lives. It felt good, I must say! I didn't know what to expect from anyone, but I knew my family would come through if I needed them to. Honestly even if I didn't need them, they would be there! That's just how my family functions; if one hurts, we all hurt, and that is literally. To many people, we may seem strange but once we let you in, the outpouring of love we give is exceptional, and sometimes you don't really know that we care about you because we can't give away all our secrets (laughing).

Naturally during my twenty-eight-day stay at the hospital, someone stayed with me every day (guardian angel and family). I was never left alone at UMMC. My mom, Sharon, and Marcia took turns staying with me. They would stay weeks at a time, never leaving my side except to go shower and exchange their visitor's badge. This was truly a blessing to have family who loved me enough to stick by my side for weeks at a time and taking time off of work to be with me. I can never thank them enough and want it publicly known that I love and appreciate everything they did for me. No matter how many hospitals stays I had during this time period, these three would always come and stay with me so that I would not be alone (tears).

I was terrified to be left alone; it was my most horrifying fear. I kept thinking, *What if no one is around when I need someone to speak, think, or even talk to me? What happens when the nurses and doctors don't see anyone visiting me frequently? I have cancer!* I was worried for nothing because my family had my back 100 percent. My mom and Sharon especially were not going to leave me alone. I was their baby! Remember, if one hurts, we all hurt; well, that's how it was for us. They would say it's something in my eyes that lets them know something is wrong; what my eyes indicated I have no idea but that's what they always said. I felt I was blessed beyond recognition and still am being blessed.

While I was in the hospital, and my family learned that I could no longer be around mold, mildew, dust, or germs, period, some of the males in my family came and redid my basement floor. They took up the carpet and put down laminated floors. The women cleaned my house from top to bottom. I already had hardwood floors upstairs, so that did not need to be replaced. My house was germ-free as much as it could be so that I could come home. My family loved me just that much that they stopped what they were doing to make sure I would be okay (tears). My heart fills with joy just knowing how much I mean to my family and they mean to me. I could not have asked God for a better family. I love my family!

After I came home, they took turns staying with me for over a year. Sometimes they would stay for two to three weeks at a time, making sure I ate, took my medicine, got plenty of rest, and made sure my children were taken care of. They did not trust that he could be there 100 percent of the time. Interesting that they knew him that well to know he would ultimately find an excuse to leave the house (sad). So they never said anything, just came and took care of my children and me. It bothered me a lot to know that my family had to step in to help me when I was married, but if it wasn't really a marriage, then why not. They did not know that, though, because I never spoke of my relationship with him. Now if I talked about it when I was high off the prescription meds, then maybe they did know; but I treated our marriage like it was the best thing since sliced bread, as the saying goes (shaking my head).

I sometimes feel that nothing can be finalized with the family if I don't give my opinion. It's not with everything, but when a mission must be complete, I'm the one to turn to. So when I needed them, they were there for me. While I was sick, they could handle things on their own, so once I became well, I didn't understand how I just picked back up where I left off. It was a little weird! It was like they were waiting for me to say I was okay to start my usual regimen (smiling). My family has shown me nothing but unconditional love through every journey that I crossed. They may be judgmental, but they do it out of love. I know they mean no harm, but I love them for their understanding. We are all getting older, and family is going to be all we have left in the end. This family's love is one for the record books because near or far, we are always there when you need us. We may complain, oh yes, but we still are there for one another with no questions asked at times.

Honestly the love you get from my family is no other love you can get from any other family because my mom taught us how to cherish our family through ups and downs. There is none like us! So when I say I put my family first, I really do because that's what I was taught. However, I also know that family can tear things apart if you let them. In any family, you must be able to have your own mind even if you have learned things a certain way. Many things, situations, circumstances are learned, and it's up to you to make it work for you, not what works for your family because at the end of the day, you must live with your decisions. That's why as a mother, I am trying to teach my children about family and encourage them to be able to think for themselves.

Motherhood: Part 2

Motherhood is a job that should be cherished and respected because it is not easy raising a family. I always say it is especially difficult for a person such as myself who never wanted children. I struggle each day with my own soul trying to figure out if I am doing the right things by my children. When I received this responsibility, I knew I would fight with my feelings because I know how hard life is and what they have in store for them, and if I don't prepare them with the proper tools, they may fail. There are many days I do not want this kind of responsibility. I love my children, without a doubt! Truthfully I don't think I would have fought so hard nor been so proud of our accomplishments. When I look at them, my heart fills with joy because all I can see is a part of me (young me, Kayla, and adult me, Layden). I am enjoying it because it gives me a reason to keep pushing myself to be better so they can have someone to look up to when or if they ever get into a situation they need a responsible person to help them make a life-changing decision.

I love my children and would not change things for the world. They are the reason I keep pushing myself even harder to be better today than I was yesterday. No, they have no idea what I am putting myself through to make sure that they are cared for, but I pray one day, they will understand that a mother's love is unconditional (even when she is upset [smile]). I always appreciated my parents, but I did not fully appreciate them until I got older and understood. They think Mommy is just being mean, but I am protecting them from what I can foresee. It's sad to say, but I am even protecting them from the ones that they even love and look up to. I know I can't control every facet of their lives, but I can place my mark so when they are faced with something, they can think about what Mommy would do or say. It's kind of funny because they say how mean I am but love me more than they show it. I know they get that from me, though, so it doesn't always bother me. They know when they need something, anything, Mommy is always right there for them.

Today I am facing more challenges because they are getting older, and I want them to be mature enough to make good decisions when it comes to friends and colleagues. I teach them that everyone is not their friend, and some that say they are their friends are talking behind their back. I try and teach them that they are their own friends and that nothing will come between them. They are always to protect each other; Kayla makes this a hard task, but she loves her little brother. It is interesting how now that they are both teenagers, their relationship is different. I guess since Layden has his own mind and thinks he is smarter than the average adult, it would be hard. He believes he is smarter than most adults!

As I watch them grow each year, I think about how I can somehow make things a little easier like my family did for me. Unfortunately these days and times, things are just so different that planning and preparing is such a task within itself. My children are taught to strategize and problem-solve situations at hand to see what is best for them. I am an older parent, so my thought process is different, and I expect more because they are a part of me. However, I know I am fighting against other aspects of their lives, and I may not always win, but I am determined to always be the last one standing. You know, people tell me that you can show your children the right way, but ultimately it is their decision on which road they will take, and there is nothing you can do about it. Well, I don't agree to dis-agree with that statement, but I can do my best to make sure that when I see them going left instead of right, they have enough respect for me to at least listen to me. I am not trying to be their friend, but I am trying to be the best mother I know how to be since I never thought I would have this opportunity. I seldom think how my life would be if I did not have Kayla and Layden, and it would probably be filled with education, education, and education because I love to learn, and I would have put all my energy in learning new things. I use to think that having children stopped you from living out your full dreams, but they just help you enhance what you already have done and give you a reason to believe that your work is worth some-thing in this world. You might not always stay together as parents, but as a mother, it is your decision on what road you will take to make sure your children are in the best place.

So when I decided to divorce him, I had to put my mother hat on as well as my health hat. I had to weigh the options because I did not want to do anything that would jeopardize my children or my health. No, divorce is never what you want, especially when you have children; but when the marriage is damaging your health where you can't focus on your children, you must act. In this world, they look at the mom when something goes wrong with the children, not the dad. Thus I had to make a decision that would break all of us down, but I would have the energy to pick us back up and set us on a track that the Lord has set for us, and it would be better than what we were facing then.

It is a little challenging, raising two children on my own, espe-cially Layden and having to say things to him more than one time. I was not raised like that because once a parent spoke to you, once you did not react, the next thing you see was either a belt or some type of reaction you would not like. He seems to think because I just yell that I am not going to do anything else to him. He is pushing my buttons, and I know he is going to push me so far, I am not going to have a choice but to react as a mother would in regard to her son. Anymore talk is cheap, actions get results! I am understanding that being a mother or parent is a tough job, but when you decide or the

Lord decides for you to bring a child into this world, you must do everything to protect, nurture, teach, and build them for their future success. We must allow them to spread their wings and explore what life has to offer them if we want to or not. They must be ready!

Therefore, I believe God knew what I needed, and He has given me the lead to fulfill my destiny in a manner that only He would know. Of course, I never wanted to get divorced or have a broken family, but when God leads me, I was always taught I must follow and never question. It may be hard, but over time, things will get easier. All I can do, as a mother, is take one day at a time and pray that I am being led by God. Let me tell you, it is not easy at all trying to be mother and father, and I tip my hat off to all the individuals who must be both parents. Just remember, God doesn't put more on us than we can bear if we just trust and believe. This is my daily prayer leading up to God's will!

LEADING UP TO GOD'S WILL

Do what is right, not what is easy.

—Unknown

God tends to reveal things to you in His own time and His own way. I believe I seen signs! So one might ask, "Where was your husband through all this, if your family was always around?" I would say he was there, but when my family was around, that was his time to take a break, so he said. With all my stays in the hospital, I believe he may have stayed all night five times. He rarely ever stayed with me to know what was really going on with me. He felt my family was supposed to keep him informed. He was my husband, so he should have been on top of things like I was when he got sick and needed me.

At first, I thought they had an agreement on my medical care and for the children, so I didn't see anything wrong with him not really being around. When they were not around, he did his best to make sure I ate, took my medicine, and got some sleep for the first six months. However, I started noticing that things weren't going as I thought they were agreed upon, so I started to try and pay more attention, which I had no idea how I was going to do that when I was so medicated to keep the pain at a minimum; but in my mind, I could. That was God! I knew when he started leaving me there with the children while I was asleep that there was a problem in paradise. He would say he was leaving them with Bria, but she was closed up in her bedroom, not even coming out to check on them. My babies were five and two years old basically, Kayla was watching us (shaking my head). Bria was just a teenager anyway, and the children were young and very active. My stepdaughter was in her own world, not worried about watching her little sister and brother!

Another sign was when the doctor first told me about not having any children while on the chemo medicine. I asked him to get a vasectomy because I was already going through a lot with fighting the cancer, and he agreed then later declined. He told me to get a tubal ligation because he wasn't letting anyone cut on him again; there was trouble in paradise. I thought this was such a selfish act, wanting me to be put to sleep while I'm going through bone marrow biopsy and fighting for my life. I just took it and went on (silent fighter).

I knew there was trouble in paradise when the doctor told me I needed a blood transfusion or I would die, and he refused, saying I could contract AIDs or HIV. The doctor told him that the chances of me getting infected would be very difficult with all the technology they use to test the blood today. But he still refused! I am glad I was sane enough to discuss my own medical treatment because he was trying to kill me (not on purpose but still). Oh my, trouble in paradise!

Then him leaving me alone with the children while I was medicated so he could go to football or basketball practice and games (so he said), there was trouble in paradise. He would be gone for hours, not even calling to check on us at times. I was so medicated I didn't even know if I was watching the children or if the children were watching me (smile). Thank God for my neighbor, Ms. Cookie and her family, because they really watched out for us when we were outside. She would sometimes ask, "Where is K going, leaving you here?" I just told her what he told me if I could remember. It got so bad that when he would say he was leaving, the children and I would just look at him in confusion because we couldn't understand why his sporting events were more important than us. The children didn't say it, but the look was enough. There was so much trouble in paradise! He just acted like everything was all right because he could get a break from us. Telling me he needed time to himself (what a man!).

The last straw for me was when my stomach had gotten so big it looked like I was nine months pregnant, and I was having shortness of breath, and he argued with me for hours before taking me to the ER. He would say, "I need a break, you are always getting sick when I want to go out of town. You just want me to be a drunk or drug addict because I am not getting any time to myself. If that's what you want, then I'll just become a drunk, and then I can be in the house all the time (mocking my father). You know I wanted to go to Las Vegas, and you decide now that you need to go to the ER." His comments were very hurtful because I was fighting for my life, and all you could do was complain about you not having time for yourself because I was always getting sick. I couldn't wrap my head around it! Why would a person who says they love you and cares about you talk and treat you this way when you are at your weakest? I just cried because I didn't know what else to do. I didn't know who else I could turn to because I needed Marilyn to watch the children while I went to the hospital.

I told him, "If I could drive myself, I would never have asked you since your trip is so important." Little did I know that the more I was getting upset and talking, the less oxygen was getting to my heart. That was the last moment there would ever be any paradise in this thing we called a marriage.

He drove me to the hospital around 9:00 p.m. or 10:00 p.m. on December 16, 2009, tipsy. When I got there, they checked me in and put me in a room to run some tests. While waiting for the results, I kept having to use the restroom. About an hour went by, and the doctor told me not to get out of bed anymore and that the doctors from upstairs would be down to see me. I could not imagine what doctors they were and why I couldn't walk to the restroom anymore. All this time, he was sitting up against the wall, asleep. I told the Lord that, "When I get well, I am getting a divorce because this man sitting on that chair does not care about me, so why am I going through all that I have been doing to keep this marriage together when it's not a marriage at all? And it's very unhealthy for me to stay where I don't belong." At that moment, the cardiologists came in and told me that my heart had water around it, and I needed to go up to ICU for a few days to release the water and get on some medication. They also said that my heart was only functioning at 10 percent, and if I would have waited any longer that I may have died. I looked at him and said to myself, *Oh hell no, this marriage is over as of this day!*

As I was getting ready to be transferred upstairs to the ICU, I couldn't help but to think that God made me sick to open my eyes to a marriage that had become toxic to my mind, body, and soul. I was always so busy that I wasn't paying attention to what was really going on in my life. There had been many, many signs, but I did not want to break up my family nor be damned to damnation for not adhering to the vows I took before God. I was just trying to do what I thought was right, but all the while I was hurting myself. Then for a moment, I thought maybe he just doesn't know how to deal with me being sick because I was always so strong. Maybe he does care but doesn't really know how to express it the right way. He possibly might not think I'm going to make it, and he would have to raise the children. Just maybe! Then I said, "Nope, he's just not who God wants for me."

He would always say that he wasn't attracted to big women, but I never thought he would feel that way when I gained weight from the steroids. Oh, was I wrong again! He didn't even want me to get the SI joint procedures because he knew the steroids were going to make me bigger. I was in excruciating pain, and all he was worried about was be gaining weight. What kind of man did I get myself hooked up with? He didn't touch me for about three years (some of it may have been because I was sick), nor did he look at me like I was still beautiful, just that I had gained some weight from my illness. Now this was it! Now let me remind you that he was 6'1", about 245–250 lbs., with a stomach and out of shape. How can you judge me and say you're not attracted to me?

That day, I made a promise to God that as soon as I felt healthy enough, I would remove myself from this toxic situation no matter what the cost. On February 11, 2011, he came in the house that morning, around 4:00 a.m., and took a shower, then got in the bed with my daughter since those where our sleeping arrangements now. Kayla stayed in the room with him, and I stayed in the room with Layden. That afternoon or early evening, as I was preparing to take my medication, I kindly asked him to leave and that our relationship was over. He got mad and said, "What, you want me out so you can move your sister or family in here?"

I replied in a calm voice, "This does not have anything to do with my family, this is between you and me."

He went on with more nonsense, and I just let him talk and went in the room with Layden and went to sleep. I felt such a relief, it was God waiting for me to do what He wanted me to do for some time now. From that day forward, I started working on getting myself healthy so that I could deal with whatever mess he may have for me. The children and I would travel back and forth to my mom's once a month so I could help take care of my brother Vernice who had been diagnosed with lung cancer in November 2010, and to get a peace of mind for the weekend. I started laughing and smiling more and feeling good about myself, even though I had gained about fifty pounds. My spirits were high because I felt free now! Then Vernice passed away on May 19, 2011, from lung cancer that had spread to his bones. He was only forty-one years old. This bothered me because I felt he didn't put up a fight like I did, and he let himself succumb to cancer.

I never expressed any of my emotions or even talked to him about anything once I asked him to leave. He did drive to Pennsylvania to be with us since we were still married, but that did not change anything in my eyes. I still wanted him gone out of my life. I was so disappointed; nothing could change my heart. He tried to suggest we go on a trip together and even counseling, but my mind was made up—I was done. His actions never changed; he was still only worried about himself while his family came second.

Before I asked him for a divorce, he suggested we work out together, but at that point, who was I doing it for—him or me? After the congestive heart failure episode, I always thought anything he suggested was for his benefit. I didn't want to benefit him, so I wouldn't participate. We became very distant, living in the same house. What a way to live, so I just always tried to stay away so my children did not have to witness anything. I felt they were too young to know what was going on or even to worry their little heads because we still loved them, even if we weren't going to be together. It took him eight months to move out but not before telling my seven-year-old daughter that I kicked him out because I didn't love him anymore. Now I felt this was very inappropriate for him to be telling her anything about what was going on except that he was moving, but he would always love her no matter where he lived. This was a very long eight months, living with someone you no longer cared for or respected. He finally moved out on October 31, 2011.

While he was still living with us, he started going back to church which I later found out he was going to his female friend's church. He would attend every Sunday but never asked to take the children. The day Kayla did ask to go, he told her "I no longer go to Eastern Community Church, but I go to a new church, and if your mom gets you dressed, you can go." Kayla never asked me, so I believe it bothered her, and she did not want to go to a different church. I believe she felt something was wrong. Why he was attending a different church with a female and he was still living with me was beyond me. If you ask him, this story will be different.

In the end, there were so many nasty acts that he was trying to see if he could hurt me, it was terrible. He knew I was not allowed or supposed to be stressed, and every time he would do something to try to set me off, I did very well until the last time he took me to court about the children, and I was ready to get arrested because he was being malicious for no reason. He should know that you never back a tiger against the wall because they will come out fighting. I had to learn how to gain an act for forgiveness.

THE ACT OF FORGIVENESS

Push yourself because, no one else is going to do it for you.

—Unknown Author

The act of forgiveness is probably the hardest action you can express. For me, forgiveness is not easy, especially when I must forgive for past and present events. I have been holding so many things, situations, actions, and mistrust inside that I don't know if I can honestly forgive. I know that it is what we are supposed to do because God forgave us, but I don't know if I can let it go. Currently it is affecting my actions, so I am going to have to set it free, but I don't really know how. I am going to need help with forgiving.

When I think about being hurt, betrayed, misrepresented, or violated, the last thing I think about is forgiveness because I have lessened my trust. Now I have my guard up for every new and old situation I encounter. Yes, I understand that I am pushing some people away, but the ones who really understand me will be there when I get myself together, if they are really concerned about me. In Ephesians 4:32, it says, "Forgive each other, just as Christ God forgave us." I grew up knowing and learning this, but when it happens to you, it's not easy to turn your head and just forgive. I know I have probably done things to individuals that I may need to ask for forgiveness, and I may expect them to forgive me. So I am a hypocrite because I want them to forgive me, but I can't forgive. It hurts to even think about forgiving. I know it is consuming my soul, and I must forgive to live a full life. I am getting better!

The Scripture is full of commands for us to love each other and overlook faults. We are reminded that love "keeps no record of wrongs" (1 Cor. 13:5), and that we should be ready to forgive one another. With God, forgiveness means that our sin is out of sight *and* out of mind. May He give us grace to extend forgiveness to those around us (Joe Stowell).

Lord, thank you for not holding my sins against me and for granting me a second chance. Help me today to forgive others just as you have so freely forgiven me.

Forgive as God forgives you—don't keep score (*Our Daily Bread* 2016). Don't keep score, huh? How can you not keep score when you are hurting? How do you forgive when you know the forgiveness will not be genuine? How can you honestly and truly forgive when you may not have forgiven yourself? There are so many different situations in which it is easier for me to forgive, but when you deliberately do things to me where I must change my personality to tackle the task, it's not a good look. I'm punishing myself for what others have done to me instead of just forgiving. I'm not ready!

This is supposed to be the days when I am cleaning out the unhealthy and consuming the healthy. Oh, how do I do that? I know I can, but I am stubborn when it comes to trying to destroy my personality or character. Yes, misery does love company! I'm not concerned with one's misery; I just worry about my well-being. I don't mind being a hypocrite, but I do want to live life free of any unnecessary consumptions from other behaviors. My soul aches for wanting to be free, but my mind can't let it go. My prayer:

> Lord, in the name of Jesus, release these emotions from my spirit and let me be free from negative consumptions. I pray for those who have wrongfully treated me for one reason or another. I pray for guidance and redemption for my soul to be able to forgive and forget. I want to be pure of unhealthy things in my mind, body, and soul. I turn my old behaviors over to you, Jesus, for you to deal with. I will not let my soul, mind, or body be consumed with others junk, and I will forgive as you have forgiven me. This is my prayer, in the name of Jesus, amen!

I forgive all those who may or may not know they have done wrong by me. I forgive you! I will not let your actions cause me any more damage, and I forgive you. I hope that you will forgive yourself as well! It is a blessing to ask for forgiveness and accept whatever the outcome. Thank you for setting my soul free so that I can rebuild my life's hopes and dreams!

REBUILDING LIFE'S HOPES AND DREAMS

(Ego Trippin')

Life is a school we never graduate from but all of us will only pass through it.

—Emmy

On November 21, 2010, I decided to take myself completely off all my medications since I wasn't taking the chemo medicine, and I didn't need my heart medicine anymore. I felt it was time for me to start getting my life back in order. I didn't tell anyone because I didn't want them to discourage me from getting myself back to good health too fast. I knew that the Lord had brought me out, so now it was time for me to start putting my life into perspective because I felt He had shown/revealed to me one of the changes I needed to fix in order for me to be happy and successful.

One of the things He revealed was that I was in a marriage that He no longer felt was healthy for me because it was draining all my energy, and I was living a lie (I still am skeptical God put this relationship together). I wasn't happy but settled because I knew God would frown on divorce, but upon the Lord's revelation, I discovered that was not the case in my situation. I had been living for others and not myself which was a big reason I stayed stressed but covered it up because I didn't want my blessings to be taken away for being disobedient to His Word regarding marriage. God revealed that if I continue in this unhealthy marriage that my blessings would not continue. I say that because the Lord gave me an illness that was curable in three years which was only enough time to open my eyes and see things for what they were and to stop covering it up. I knew but I accepted it as it was because I thought that was the right thing to do and not be a statistic. He had other aspirations for me, so did God put us together or did I allow man to control me once again?

When I was diagnosed, I weighed 179 lbs. I did not lose any weight through this whole fight but gained weight. I was the heaviest cancer patient, I thought, ever to exist. I got up to 225 lbs. from the steroids that were being injected for the bone marrow biopsy and the narcotic pain medication I was prescribed. Kelvin did not like me being big! He would try to get me to go to the gym because he was not attracted to big women because he was a big man. I was his wife, and I was going through a traumatic experience, so why judge me. He made comments that the medication fried my brain because he wasn't acting the way I was seeing it. Wow, what heartache! He had not touched me intimately for about two years or more. One day, I asked him why he hadn't touched me, and he said because he is not attracted to big women. I was big, so I was in that category now. This really hurt, I must say, and took me for a loop.

So once I did not need the bone marrow biopsy so frequently, I changed the narcotic medication to nonnarcotic medicine in January 2011. I started losing all the water weight and got down to 210 lbs. in about thirty days. Then it just started coming down. I was on another mission now—to show him that I may be big on the outside, but I am beautiful inside and out. So I started working and building up my self-esteem to leave his superficial self. He was selfish, and he just proved it repeatedly, so why do I need to stay?

I had picked back up on training and coaching through my consulting business. It's amazing how I only stopped working for about one year, and I was back at it (silent fighter). I was a little unsure about myself and my decisions, but I did not let anyone know my weakness. I acted like I had everything together, regardless as to what I was feeling on the inside. I just thought I had to somehow get out of this unhealthy marriage, and if I had to go back to work sooner than I was supposed to, I had to do what I had to do because

I couldn't help thinking my husband did not care about my well-being, just his. I was done with this relationship!

On January 3, 2011, I reached out to an old friend I had lost contact with for thirteen years because I needed a true friend who wasn't in my current inner circle who could be encouraging and supportive—what I needed at that point because I thought I was going crazy. We spoke for about four hours, just conversing about life and its ups and downs, nothing personal. I never revealed that my marriage or life was in shambles, I just needed a friend who would listen and not judge. After our long conversation, I knew I had the strength to overcome all my present obstacles and to look forward to a long life of celebrations and happiness. I had my energy to restore! Thank you, best friend (smile)!

RESTORING YOUR ENERGY

Sometimes you have to give up on people, not because you don't care, but because they don't.

—Unknown

When he moved out on October 31, 2011, I thought that day would never come. Even though I was getting advice from others about different things he was putting me through, I just went with my heart and not all the advice. Yes, there were somethings I didn't know or think about, but I wanted to do what was best for my children since they were only four and seven years old. I wanted them to live normal childhoods, even though their dad would not be in the same house.

That was short-lived because he was telling Kayla grown folks' stuff which, in turn, had an impact on her in school and socially. He introduced my children to his girlfriend, not even a month after he moved out of my house. I was so angry with him and his bad decision-making when it came to our children. Children are innocent until an adult breaks their innocence, and that's what I believe he did to Kayla. He was placing Kayla in situations I never would think he would have done, but I was wrong. He was testing me!

He wanted to talk to the children together, but I just felt they were too young to worry about what we were doing as adults. Layden would not have understood, but I did forget about Bryan and Bria and how they would feel. But that's their biological father, so he had the upper hand. Kayla understood a little bit, but she just knew her daddy wasn't going to be living with us, and he should have kept it at that with no personal comments which would affect her.

On July 21, 2012, he took me to court, saying I committed adultery because I told him that (now who goes to court on a he-said-she-said theory). Oh, I know—Kelvin! Although he was the one living with his girlfriend but using a different address (huh?), I did not say anything, though (shaking my head). The judge denied it anyway because he did not have evidence, just me telling him (dumb move). I didn't understand why he couldn't wait, and he would jeopardize my character on a court document (selfish). Even when he told me he was filing for a divorce, I never thought that it was because of adultery. When he told me it was for adultery, I was blown. Who does that anymore (especially a man)? He always let others convince him of things, so I was sure his girlfriend had something to do with it (crazy). I just couldn't imagine why he would do something like that for our children to inquire about it when they became adults. That would not look good for either one of us on a court document (shamed).

I really could not believe he thought I would do something like that because I was trying to get my life in order without him in it. Everyone knows you can't go by word of mouth in the court of law without actual proof, and why would I agree to something like that anyways? I knew he wanted a divorce, but hell, not more than I did. He took my prime years away from me; I wanted out just as bad, but I would have not warped his character to do so knowing that one day, the children may inquire about our divorce papers. I guess I am and always was the better person! The judge denied it, and we had to wait until October 31, 2012, to file for an absolute divorce. He hurried up and did file. So I also filed for child support, even though I was not a strong believer (and still skeptical) of the child support system; but after the actions he was expressing, I did not want to have to deal with it. By having the court take it out, it would be much easier for the both of us, and no hard feelings will ever be in question. I did not do it to have the courts in our business, I just wanted to not have to deal with it as time went on.

Contrary to what he may believe, I never did anything to distort his character to the children or anyone else. I felt just because it did not work out for us does not mean I would just drag his name in the mud. I have children with this man, and I must respect them, if no one else. Yes, I got much backlash for this, but I was doing what I thought was best for the sake of my children. If I was to be bitter, that would make it difficult on my children, and I never wanted that for them. They are my heart, and I will not do anything to hurt them for anyone!

We were granted our divorce after fifteen and a half years together on January 22, 2013. It was bittersweet, but in a way, I know that this is just a part of the plan God has prepared for me. To those of us who really listen to God's Word, I heard what He was saying to me. We think He leads us a little way, then we detach for a minute, not realizing what we have done. He stops us right in our tracks and turns us around, only if we are listening and ready to hear His Word. This was what I did to make sure I was making the right choice with divorcing a man who was not healthy for me. He was not the choice God had for me, but he still is the father of my children, and I must do all that I can to make sure I do not taint their feeling about him. I want them to find out on their own who their father really is. They love him, and I am not going to stand in the way unless I see harm coming their way.

In some ways, I think the divorce has affected Kayla, but since she doesn't really talk to me about many of the things that bother her, I will not know until she opens up to me (she is starting to with no filter). It bothers me that she probably still holds me accountable for the breakup, but I pray one day, she will see it was for the good. I never wanted my actions to affect my children, but sometimes, you must do what's best for you and what God has planned for you. I have no regrets!

With this divorce, I want to make sure my children never second-guess themselves when it comes to making such a major decision. I am teaching them to trust themselves and no one else. This experience has been a journey for my children and me. I believe we will grow and enjoy what pleasures God has in store for us. In the Bible, divorce is looked upon as a sin, but only if God has put you together, I believe. In addition, God does not want you to suffer, that's why Jesus came to save us from our sins. My faith and my friendships are what has been keeping me and is bringing me through this ordeal without a lot of stressors or headaches.

WHAT ARE FRIENDS FOR!

Don't let me end my journey without mentioning five special friendships I have gained in my adult life. They are Kamila, Eddie, LaRone, Dorothy, and Michael. These five friendships have, in their own manner, helped me lift my spirits and set higher goals for myself. They are my support team!

I met Kamila in 2005 while working on the pre-K incentive pilot program in DC, and we have been like sisters ever since. She was my angel when I didn't know how I was going to make it through my divorce, going through remission, finding consulting work, and much more. She would just come over to the house and visit just because, and it was usually at the perfect time. Kamila never let her relationship with him come between our friendship/sister bond because she was my friend. She would never let me allow his negativity to ruin my beauty and wanted me to start showing my outer beauty as well as my inner beauty more. Her encouragement was phenomenal. Kamila was very encouraging in helping me expose my sensual beauty from looking like, as she called it, an old lady to expressing my sexiness no matter my size (smile). She has been my *rock* in the middle of a storm, and I *thank* and *love* her for that and much more!

Eddie, on the other hand, I have known since 1991. Because we are both from Pennsylvania, we have certain moral and values we expect. He has made himself family (smile) from living with my sister to finding his own way in this DMV area. He has always had my back no matter what! I am a handful sometimes, and he would just ignore me and tell me what I needed to hear. Eddie has always

241

been straight to the point no matter if I want him to or not. We are quite opposites (laughing), and he makes me think more outside the box (like I really need to). He's the one who shows tough love but in a subtle way. Eddie has very good intentions and is a wonderful friend. Even though we don't talk much, I can tell he's looking out for me. I *thank* him and love him for being there when I thought no one was listening or being supportive!

Now LaRone is a gentleman I met through Kayla's friend, Kirsten. He is a quiet, playful, and humorous man with a loving heart (military man). He has been helping me even when I was still married with my children. LaRone and I have never really shared personal information about each other, but somehow, we became friends. He would do things and never complain or say a word for my children. He just has this way about himself that makes it easy to trust him. Our daughters are our common denominator, but I do consider him as a special friend because if I needed a listening ear, he wouldn't say anything, just listen. He gives me advice about the children, and I do the same for him. LaRone has been a silent friend for me, and he probably doesn't even know it (smile)! I *thank* and love him for being such a blessing to me and my children!

Dorothy and my friendship is business and personal. I met her in 2006 when she had her pre-K incentive program, and she needed assistance with maintaining her records. Kamila and I agreed to help her since we understood how the program was to be managed. I worked with her for a few months. Since then, we had lost touch until August 2011, when I had taken my niece Tara to the emergency room at children's hospital, and she was there with her daughter. She told me she had been looking for me to help her go through national accreditation. So I agreed. Dorothy had known all about my illness and knew I could not devote a lot of time, but I would do what I could until I was well enough, but she just wanted my expertise no matter what. Over time, we have not only been supportive of the program but also supportive of each other and became like family. She understood my limits from the beginning, and when I was going through my personal issues, she was right there to lend an ear or give advice. Dorothy has been very good to me, and I *thank* and love her for being so understanding and caring (smile).

How can I describe Michael and me? As you have read, we have history together. We had no contact from 1997–2011. I thought about how he was doing, but I would never ask because I did not know why he ever stopped speaking to me in the first place. So when I did finally reach out (character change), it was like we never stopped being friends. We always took pride in being friends before anything else because that's how we really came to know each other. Yes, he grew up beside my cousin Carrie, but I never really paid him any attention because he was younger than us. As time went on, we became friends (it was so easy talking to him and maybe because we have things in common). Michael is my best friend no matter what! Our intellect and aspirations are so much alike, sometimes I think I am looking in the mirror. When I found out we still had feelings for each other, it was shocking (wide eyes). All the time that had passed, and there were still emotions that had never been resolved (smile). He also made me feel good about myself through everything (and still does). It's interesting how we help each other. We were young and did not know what we wanted, and now that we are older, it sometimes stills seems that way. However, I did encourage him to move from Pennsylvania because his dreams are too big for that place, and he would be more successful in a larger city. I believe God has a plan for us, and only we can help fulfill the plan. No matter if we stay best friends or make things official, I don't think anything will break our friendship and love. I love this man and thank him for everything. I tell him all the time, I don't know if anyone besides us would understand our relationship (laughing).

Now let me live out my dreams!

LIVING OUT MY DREAM

Ordinary riches can be stolen; real riches cannot. In your soul are infinitely precious things that cannot be taken from you.

—Oscar Wilde

In September 2014, I became the founder and owner of Legendary Leaders for Tomorrow, LLC with my trade name Legendary Leaders Institute in Maryland. I have been self-employed since 2008, but I am now officially branded. In 2014 alone, I have obtained an American Red Cross Instructor's Certificate to train on first aid/CPR/AED, Prometric Proctor Certification to train as a certified professional food manager (food handler), and started working on becoming a GED preparatory instructor, Maryland child care certification trainer, and DC certified trainer (individual).

I am looking forward to opening my own professional, business, and educational institute in the near future. I want to reach as many people as I can through encouragement, support, and positive guidance so they can look at the future more seriously. I especially want to help our young black boys and girls to see that their lives do have a meaning, and there is a purpose. I would eventually like to work with all young boys and girls starting in the seventh grade in urban areas, letting them know that there is a world out there beyond their current environments, just waiting for them to capture. I know this will not be easy, but I am in it for the long haul.

In 2020, I plan to open Little Legends Nannie Agency as well as Humble Hearts Healthcare. These two business ventures will open more doors for me to help my children when they become adults and family who are looking to start their own business because these both can become franchises for the family. This will also help me with my clinical psychology practice because I will already have possible clients that I can move into a clinic. Since Kayla wants to be a psychiatric nurse practitioner and Layden something in technology, I believe by the time they are ready, I will have access to helping own their own practice and business.

I am still struggling with aspects of my life and family, but it is not going to stop me from reaching my goals. One thing, I do not look at others' accomplishments and compare them to mine. I believe God gives you what you need when He feels you are ready to accept it. What may look like a blessing on the outside may not be such a blessing on the inside. So don't judge a book by its cover because there may not be a spine holding it together! I have faith enough to believe that my God" has already worked my situations out, and I just need to do my part in making *our* plan a true testimony. I am going to remember how to win!

Remembering How to Win

*Be who you were created to be and
you will set the world on fire.*

—St. Catherine of Sienna

So I decided, since I was getting a second chance in life, that I was going to enjoy it and not be so serious all the time. It felt like I was on cloud 9, just free-spirited. I began hanging with my girlfriends more and getting out of the house. I started losing all that water weight without trying. I was thinking more positively, and I made sure I kept an encouraging and supportive network of close friends and family. I had three main supporters as friends who kept me grounded and encouraged. Since Kelvin felt I was too big for him and that the medicine had fried my brain, I had these three close individuals who would tell me differently. They were there if I needed to talk, advice, share stories, or even just to hang out. I will always love, respect, and appreciate them for that. It was a difficult time, but I promised myself I wouldn't let him see me sweat over anything that he did, so I confided in one of these three. It made things easier for me!

The separation took me for a twist because he was acting like a woman would act when they are scorned. I started questioning his actions because they did not seem right to me. I know I may have hurt him with some of my words, but his actions and words hurt me long before I could have ever hurt him. I am not the type to get back at people for wrongs they have done to me because I feel that is God's place to judge. However, when it comes to you hurting my children, I have a major problem. So this is where the problems begin with my children.

He did so many things that were inappropriate from the time he was still living with us until we were divorced (in my eyes). I always

246

thought that when you have children, you do not introduce them to other parties until you think they are ready, and you see it may be serious. As an educator, I know the impact it has on children when parents bring third parties into the picture too early and too often. Sometimes it can be detrimental to a child, and I believe until today, Kayla has been affected by his poor decision-making. I am not saying I am perfect, but I thought about my children first before I made any decisions going through this separation and, ultimately, divorce.

I moved on as well, but I did not bring anyone around my children until we were almost divorced. What I did was my business, not my children's. I did not want my children to be scorned or see different people in and out of our lives, so when I selected the right person, that was who was introduced to my children, and I am still with him now. I do not know if we will ever be married, but I do know that I am remembering that winning feels good. When you have a person in your life who believes in you just as much as you believe in them, and you are equally yoked, or at least on the same page mentally, spiritually, and emotionally. These are the people who matter, therefore, you are *winning*! Life is too short to miss all your opportunities that are placed before you, so we have to rise to the occasion and just keep winning, pushing, pulling, praising, and pressing on to that great place or places in which we belong. Do not stop winning because these things really matter!

WHO REALLY MATTERS?

Life is too short for fake butter, cheese or people.

—Unknown

During this time, I did get Kayla back on track with school (somewhat), but it is a struggle socially and emotionally for her, and I really don't know how to fix it. I pray time will heal! Yes, in my eyes, he tried to distort me to Kayla, and maybe Layden too; but Layden is young, so he doesn't fully understand yet. I feel that I should have justified myself a little when he was telling her things, but I felt that was not for her little precious ears and mind to be focusing on. My way of protecting her may have hurt, but I did what I thought was best at the time. It hurts me knowing that she had to suffer through this by no means of her own, but she loved her daddy, and he did no wrong until she wanted him to be around more (smile). She is seeing things more clearly now that she is older, but I believe if I would have acted in a different manner, my children would not be honor students and excelling today. It takes a strong person to do what I did!

Remember, I was still going through remission while dealing with all this divorce stuff. Him taking me to court five times over the course of five years over things to do with the children and for our divorce. Just anything to try to get to me! However, I was not to be stressed because it could have triggered the cancer to return or something else. It was best for me to just stay prayed up and covered in the blood of Jesus. So that's what I did! No, it wasn't easy at all, but it helped me cope with situations that were placed in my path. If you put your mind to it, you can do anything! I had to for the sake of my children because they are who really matters! They are my everything!

I even became the secretary of the school PTA in 2013–2014 because LaRone was asked to become the president, and he needed a secretary (which everyone knows that is not a strong skill of mine), so he confided in me. I really did it for him and nothing else because I was a busy little lady. For all that he has helped me with, that was the least I could do for him. It was a hard year, but we got it together, and we both only did one term but left it in good hands. I only did it because he asked, and I kept my word even for as busy as I was at times! I believe our friendship is good enough that we respect each other enough to do that for each other. Now they want me to run as president because some feel I can make it grow and be very successful. I guess how the saying goes, "people are watching you when you don't even know it." We will have to see, but I did not run the next year! Honestly politics is not my strong suit, so that wasn't a real calling for me. I can support but not run for a school PTA, at least. I may do it in the future, if I see fit, for the sake of my children.

As you will see in the "Today" chapter, I am living my life differently and really trying to hold on to those friends who have been there for me through everything. You may find that some have come at different times, but they all play a major role in helping me be a better person and mother. I have learned to appreciate having friends and colleagues. You cannot raise children on your own or fight a good fight on your own. Positive support and a helping hand go a long way! I have great, blessed, honorable people around me who matter more to me more than they can ever imagine. Our bond is like mold that holds no matter what, and I am so appreciative for it! I may never get another chance or opportunity to find great people I have in my life, so I am going to take chances.

I have found that God is putting so many people in my life that are blessed and blessings that I do not want to lose. He is giving me what matters the most! I cannot have asked for anything more. I have learned how to take chances and not being scared to fail because without failure, there is no success. It took people who matter to teach me this! I am not taking anything for granted, so let's see what's happening today.

TODAY'S WORLD

Life is a puzzle; sometimes it is tough sometimes it is simple; sometimes you find your way, sometimes you simply lose your say, but, everything left per say, the puzzle has to be solved, everyone has to lay, life is truly a puzzle per say!

—wishafriend.com

Don't waste your time looking back on what you've lost. Move on for life is not meant to be travelled backwards.

—Unknown Author

It's not about getting a chance, it's about taking a chance.

—Unknown

Today I am living life to the fullest! I received a second chance, and I am taking it in strides. Although going through this ordeal helped me open my eyes to who I really am and who I really represent in this thing we call life. I recall always living my life for my family, especially my mom, because I never wanted to be a disappointment. So I basically lived for others and let others live through me for many years. It wasn't until my third year of remission that I realized I didn't even know how to make myself happy. Scary, huh?

In sharing my story, I was asked, "What makes you happy?" And I couldn't answer it because I just did things. I always felt happiness is what you make it, so I was always happy if those I love were happy. However, that wasn't the case because I really wasn't happy, just empty inside. You know the statement or saying you are surrounded by people but lonely inside. That was me! Yes, I love my children and family, but something was missing inside. I do so much for so many people that my soul is empty (wondering). This is new!

It wasn't until my thirty-seventh birthday that I honestly got real with myself and acknowledged my happiness (but is it happiness?). Yes, I was in remission, going through a divorce, taking on single parenthood, and embarking on my own business ventures. But what better time to find out who you are and what makes you happy? I believe that simple things make me happy such as being surrounded—not literally—by the one's I love, having moments to be alone, acts of kindness, spending time with my children, and finding the love of my life (which he was a past love, but we were young at the time to really know what was best for us). I never saw myself as a person needing to be genuinely loved by a man, but not having my marriage be completely designed for what God had in store for me made me realize I wasn't being completely honest with myself. I do want to be loved unconditionally and not be alone. For me, companionship is necessary for my happiness. Sometimes I think I conduct psychology on myself (smile) because it helps make me human and understand my own feelings and perceptions.

My happiness has allowed me to look to a more exciting and fulfilled future, but not so much that I will allow my heart to cloud my judgment. I have been there and done that! I do not want to fall in a trap ever again when it comes to opening my heart to someone who doesn't deserve me. I believe God places individuals in your path at the right times, but not to let your current situation cloud what you really need to see. When you look at me, you would never know what triumphs I had faced in my forty-plus years here on earth. Many people tell me my life is a living testimony, and I am a walking miracle but learning that my name means "God is gracious" is a blessing to me because He has placed a special guardian angel over me to lead me through my journey in life. It is not easy at all, but I am doing my best and trying to bring people along for the ride as well. My eyes always have seen something different, but I never let my heart get close enough to see what I am seeing.

I made a promise to my mom that when I make it to my fifth-year anniversary that I would write a book as a testimony as to how good my God is and that's what I am doing. It has taken me a couple more years to sit down and write it since my fifth anniversary was on January 14, 2014, but I am keeping my promise. It is time now!

There are things I have done that I am not very proud of, but it seems they are things that I needed to do at that time to help me become who I am. As the saying goes, "don't count the skeletons I have, just make sure yours are in order." A very logistical expression, I think! Yes, books all have covers, but what would a book be without a spine, just pages with no true meaning? I never want my life to be pages with no meaning, so I will do whatever I have to do to make sure my spine is safely secured.

As of June 2014, I have helped build relationships (business and personal), gained more respect, empowered more people to think positively about their situations and lives, I'm looked upon as a testimony for others who may have traveled or will travel in my path to look to the light with your heart and not see the darkness with your eyes. I believe I have touched people just by them seeing how I have overcome so many obstacles in so little time.

I am on this journey to a new faith that I never knew I had confidence. In my life, it always just seemed like God was always showing up no matter what the situation (good or bad) which has helped me gain my confidence and compassion for others, my family, and life itself. It has been eleven and a half years since I was diagnosed, and now it feels as though I have come to a crossroad with my faith, career, and family. I seem to be carrying more on my shoulders than I should. I am more emotional, sympathetic, arrogant, demanding, and opinionated now. Although so many feel I have always been arrogant and opinionated (smile). I believe now I know what I want and press on daily to make sure it happens because I could not foresee it before. Don't believe for a minute that finding out who I am has been easy because it has been far from easy. When you look at yourself in the mirror and admit your faults, it is scary because on the outside, you have one look, but on the inside, you are another person. Beauty is on the inside; but if you are blessed with them both, do not misuse them or abuse them. God has blessed you with a gift that you should never take for granted!

So as you can see, I still have much more work to be done, and I plan on doing everything I can to accomplish it. No more mountain I can't climb over, no more earthquakes I can't stop, no more villages I can't help, and no more excuses! I am not scared to do whatever it is that needs to be done for my faith that God will see me through. Fear has never stopped me from doing my good work, just skepticism (human mind) which is not one of my characteristics. So continue to challenge me!

Note: my family is very important to me but being able to live my life as I want to nowadays is more important to me. I know with every breath I take is another opportunity God has given me to live, conquer, and be a testimony to someone. I take pride in this gift and will do all that I can to make it a reality. God is not finished with me yet, and I look forward to the many things I will experience along this path He has made for me. We will see how it turns out!

To Be Continued

BIBLIOGRAPHY

Chemocare.com. "Arsenic Trioxide." (2015). http://chemocare.com/chemotherapy/drug-info/arsenic-trioxide.aspx.

Chemocare.com. "ATRA." (2015). http://chemocare.com/chemotherapy/drug-info/atra.aspx.

Cystic Fibrosis Foundation. "Vascular Access Devices: PICCs and Ports." (2006). https://www.cff.org/Life-With-CF/Treatments-and-Therapies/Medications/Vascular-Access-Devices-PICCs-and-Ports/.

Familydoctor.org. "Breech Babies: What Can I Do If My Baby Is Breech?" (2015). https://familydoctor.org/tag/external-cephalic-version/.

"Forgive as God Forgives You—Don't Keep Score." *Our Daily Bread*. (2016).

Genetic Home Reference. "Acute Promyelocytic Leukemia." (March 2015). https://ghr.nlm.nih.gov/condition/acute-promyelocytic-leukemia.

Grace. Merriam-Webster-Dictionary.com. (2016). www.merriam-websterdictionary.com.

MedLine Plus. "Daunorubicin." (2015). https://medlineplus.gov/druginfo/meds/a682289.html.

Recover-from-grief.com. "Seven Stages of Grief." (2107). https://www.recover-from-grief.com/7-stages-of-grief.html.

Veritashealth.com. "SI Joints." (2015). https://www.spine-health.com/glossary/sacroiliac-joint-dysfunction.

WebMD. "Understanding MRSA Infection—the Basics." (2015). https://www.webmd.com/skin-problems-and-treatments/understanding-mrsa#1.

Wikipedia. "Acute Myeloid Leukemia (AML)." (February 2015). https://en.wikipedia.org/wiki/Acute_myeloid_leukemia.

ABOUT THE AUTHOR

LaShawn J. Tracy is a survivor of APL, congestive heart failure, and divorce. She is a self-made entrepreneur in many areas, but her focus is education. LaShawn is an inspirational, motivational, spiritual, and devotional person. Her testimony to her character is captured throughout this book and shows you how she continues to strive and walk with grace, regardless of setbacks. She is resilient and has plenty of grit to share with others. LaShawn is the mother of two children and will be fulfilled when she obtains her doctorate in clinical psychology. She puts faith first in everything she does.